THE
WORLD GOLF
HALL OF FAME

1998

American Golfer titles may be purchased for business or promotional use for special sales. For information, please write to: Mr. Vince Laurentino, The American Golfer, Inc., 151 Railroad Avenue, Greenwich, Connecticut 06830.

The AMERICAN GOLFER and its logo, its name in scripted letters, are trademarks of The American Golfer, Inc.

FIRST EDITION

ISBN 1-888531-04-5

Published by:
The American Golfer, Inc.
151 Railroad Avenue
Greenwich, Connecticut 06830
(203) 862-9720
(203) 862-9724 FAX
IMD@aol.com

Designed by:
ALL CAPS Design
599 Riverside Avenue
Westport, Connecticut 06880
(203) 221-1609

Art Direction and Design by:
NK Design
154 Parsons Drive
Hempstead, New York 11550
(516) 485-1610
(516) 485-1626 FAX

Film and Separations by:
Color Associates
10818 Midwest Ind. Blvd.
St. Louis, MO 63132
(314) 423-8080

ACKNOWLEDGMENTS
Grateful appreciation to the World Golf Foundation and The World Golf Hall of Fame for allowing us to publish this book. Much thanks to Ruffin Beckwith, Helen Atter, Jerri Moon and Karen Bednarski for their active assistance, encouragement and help.

A very special thanks to John Morris, Vice President of Communications of the PGA TOUR, without whose editorial assistance and guidence this book could not have been published. Thanks as well to Cathy Lewis, Wes Seeley, Dave Lancer and John Snow, also of the PGA TOUR, for their invaluable assistance.

Thanks to Marty Parkes, Maxine Vigliotta and Nancy Stulack of the USGA, Larry Hasak and the Muirfield Village Golf Club and the communications staff of the LPGA Tour for providing much of the artwork used in this book.

Much appreciation as well to Sal Johnson for checking all of the statistics in this book and to Don Wade for providing another set of eyes on the manuscript.

Last, and certainly not least, thanks to our terrific art director, Nancy Koch of NK Design.

Photo Credits:
Table of Contents, © Brian Morgan.

Other golf books by The American Golfer:

The Hogan Mystique

The Greatest of Them All: The Legend of Bobby Jones

Byron Nelson: The Story of Golf's Finest Gentleman and The Greatest Winning Streak In History

The 25 Greatest Achievements in Golf

THE PLAYERS Championship: 25th Anniversary

Classic Instruction

THE
WORLD GOLF
HALL OF FAME

1998

BY JAIME DIAZ, TIM ROSAFORTE AND MARTIN DAVIS

The American Golfer, Inc. ■ 151 Railroad Avenue ■ Greenwich, CT 06830 ■ tel. 203-862-9720 ■ fax: 203-862-9724

Contents

Building the World Golf Village and Hall of Fame

"It's amazing how many people have bought into this vision. It's been an extraordinary collaboration on so many levels..."

— RUFFIN BECKWITH

It was eight weeks before the grand opening, about 30 months since the groundbreaking, and Ruffin Beckwith was in his office, looking at an aerial slide of the World Golf Village in the days before it was the World Golf Village — before the PGA TOUR brought together all the major golf organizations to form what is being called "the most ambitious project ever undertaken in golf."

Today, the World Golf Foundation and the World Golf Hall of Fame have the support of everybody from the AJGA to the USGA, a list of 26 associations, foundations and organizations that came together for the good of the game. Originally planned as a PGA TOUR Hall of Fame, the project has grown to include the entire world of golf.

"We had nothing to sell but a dream," said Beckwith, the Executive Director of

Illustration by James F. Earl

the World Golf Hall of Fame.

Beckwith remembered flying over this property when he first got his pilot's license, taking off from St. Augustine Airport in a two-seat Cessna and following Interstate 95 to Jacksonville. Back then this was just another indistinguishable parcel of Florida land. That was less than three years ago. He remembered the day they had a ribbon-cutting ceremony to commemorate the building of the Interstate interchange. And he remembered when developer Jim Davidson told him about hunting wild pig and turkey on this land. It was as if Deane Beman, then Commissioner of the PGA TOUR, was saying, "Build it, and they will come," when he devised the idea of a PGA TOUR Hall of Fame almost a decade ago — but not even Deane's peek-into-the-future vision foresaw the enormity of this golf landmark.

"This wasn't the sexiest piece of property in the world," said Beckwith. "It's not exactly the Monterey Peninsula. It was rural and undeveloped. There was no interchange, just a dirt road that led to this big, square pit. That's all there was."

Now there is a pond with an island green, and the two-lane country road that was known as Nine Mile Road has become a four-lane thoroughfare called International Golf Parkway. The first of three golf courses, "The Slammer & The Squire," is up and running. The 75,000-square foot World Golf Hall of Fame and IMAX theatre are nearing completion and workers are putting furniture in the 300-room World Golf Village Resort Hotel and St. Johns County Convention Center. Beckwith thought: It wasn't long ago that hotel builder John Q. Hammons stood on almost this same spot and had the vision to see the forest through the trees.

"Now let me see if I understand this," Hammons said. "You want me to build a four-or five-star hotel a two-week mule ride from Jacksonville? I'm just old

enough, rich enough and crazy enough to do it."

On May 19, 1998, when the World Golf Hall of Fame and Village officially opened to the public, there were no mule rides being offered down the Walk of Champions. In 1999, nearly 1 million people are expected to take Exit 95A off the interstate and turn into the World Golf Village, and what they will find is one of the most remarkable stories in golf, development, business and theme entertainment. When it's built out, when the final house is sold, this will be a $1 billion project, with 7,200 homes, 400-plus vacation ownership villas, over 400,000 square feet of shops, galleries, restaurants and boutiques, plus components such as a golf academy, a golf

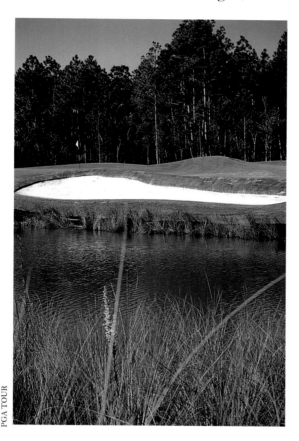

The first course at the World Golf Village, "The Slammer & The Squire," is named in honor of Sam Snead and Gene Sarazen. From the back tees, it plays to 6,940 yards, but features five sets of tees to accommodate players of all skill levels.

library and a full-service spa.

This is an interactive 21st century model not only for Halls of Fame, but for communities and destination vacation resorts. You can hit balls to an island green. You can have a cyberchat with the Hall of Famers. You can have dinner at a number of different restaurants or shop at the PGA TOUR Stop, a 30,000 square-foot retail store. You can learn what Old Tom Morris and Young Tom Watson once had in common, and you can compare your swing to Tiger Woods and Greg Norman.

"It's amazing how many people have bought into this vision," Beckwith said. "It's been an extraordinary collaboration on so many levels, but that's what it takes to build something like this from absolutely ground zero."

Beckwith has been involved with golf most of his life. His father was an owner of *Golf World*, and as a photographer for that magazine, he lived in Pinehurst, N.C., site of the old World Golf Hall of Fame. When he left the Ladies Professional Golf Association in New York and drove to Florida in 1982 to work in the PGA TOUR's Communications Department, he made a bunch of notes, outlining the plans for what he called The American Golf Museum. The LPGA's Hall of Fame didn't really physically exist. Golf House was in Far Hills, N.J. The World Golf Hall of Fame was struggling in Pinehurst.

"It was fun to think about, but at the time naive and idealistic, so I didn't share it with anyone," Beckwith said. "I never actually believed it could happen."

It has happened right before his eyes. From his office on the third floor of the PGA TOUR Productions Building, Beckwith thought about the time-lapse sequence of pictures that would show the before and after of this immense project, one taken every few hours since the tower went up, all 170 feet of it, from the banks of what used to be a pit.

"We didn't do this and all of a sudden it appeared." — DEANE BEMAN

On Sept. 11, 1974, Deane Beman attended the opening ceremonies of the World Golf Hall of Fame in Pinehurst. President Gerald R. Ford was there to dedicate the facility and take part in the ceremonies that honored the eight living and five deceased members of the World Golf Hall of Fame. Gene Sarazen, Ben Hogan, Byron Nelson, Sam Snead, Patty Berg, Arnold Palmer, Gary Player, Jack Nicklaus were all in attendance. "Golf has needed a Hall of Fame for some 50 to 75 years," Hogan said in his induction speech. "And the World Golf Hall of Fame is a great tribute to golf and to those of us who play it."

Beman had become TOUR Commissioner that March, succeeding Joe Dey. It was a moving and memorable occasion, but Beman ultimately felt the PGA TOUR needed its own Hall of Fame to honor the careers of players who might not eventually qualify for the World Golf Hall of Fame. He also knew, as time passed, that the World Golf Hall of Fame was losing money, and that Pinehurst's lack of accessibility had hurt it.

The problem was that the PGA of America had control of the World Golf Hall of Fame. Beman didn't want to drag his feet, but he also didn't want to wait on the PGA to decide what it was going to do with Pinehurst — so he went ahead and did his own thing.

The TOUR had established its headquarters at Ponte Vedra Beach in 1979, and one year later opened the Tournament Players Club at Sawgrass Stadium course. Beman got 400 acres for that project for $1 by convincing Paul and Jerome Fletcher that it would be a tremendous investment for their surrounding property to have the PGA TOUR's flagship course and a tele-

vised tournament. The Fletcher brothers held title to more than 7,000 acres on which the previous owner had planned to develop a 50,000-unit mobile retirement home community. The Fletchers were interested in finding a "special" element to enhance what they planned as an upscale residential community. And today Ponte Vedra Beach and Sawgrass are among the premier golf communities in America.

Beman's standard operating procedure as Commissioner was to create projects and assign staff to execute them. The Hall of Fame project became a priority for Tim Finchem when he joined the PGA TOUR staff as Vice President of Business Affairs in 1987 and Finchem's role increased when he became the TOUR's Deputy Commissioner and Chief Operating Officer in 1989.

Beman and Finchem knew that the beaches were not a place for the PGA TOUR Hall of Fame, so they had Vernon Kelly, the TOUR's President of Golf Course Properties, scout a piece of property near the juncture of Interstate 95 and Interstate 295 called the Appelbaum Trust/Julington-Durban Creek Peninsula. The TOUR had an option on the 2,700

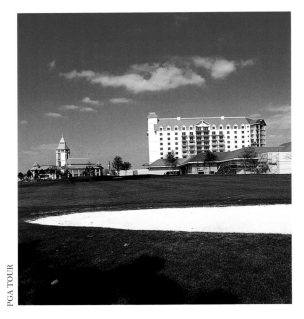

The 300-room World Golf Village Resort Hotel and Convention Center.

acres, but this occurred during a time when the environmental criteria to define Florida's wetlands was in a period of transition. When it became apparent that it would take three years before the issue was settled, the TOUR had to pass on the deal. Ultimately this turned out to be a blessing.

Beman and Finchem were set on the I-95 corridor, because it was a gateway into one of the world's largest tourist destinations. To be able to tap into 10 million of the 42 million who come to Florida every year created a built-in audience that Pinehurst never had. The next step, and the most important, was to create an experience that was fun, and one that not just the avid golfers would enjoy. It had to appeal to people who had a passing fancy, or a developing interest in the game. "We had to have a facility that addressed all that," said Kelly. "It couldn't be static, something with just balls and implements and pictures. It had to be interactive, in order to keep the attention of people who weren't interested in golf. That meant spending a lot of money."

The way Kelly and the TOUR saw the financing work was the same way it structures its TPC deals — that is, identify and target investors who would benefit from an association, and have them share the costs of the project. The first stop had been the city of Jacksonville, and the office of Senior Executive officer Richard Bowers. "Any local government would kill for a chance to have that in their jurisdiction," Bowers said. But when the Appelbaum Trust fell through, the TOUR became hard-pressed to find a suitable piece of property in Duval County. It wasn't long afterward that Bowers left the city to become the TOUR's Vice President for Community Affairs, and later he would become a key player in making the World Golf Village happen.

Just to the south in St. Johns County, in the northwest corner of greater St. Augustine, there was a 6,300-acre parcel called Saint Johns Harbor that was already per-

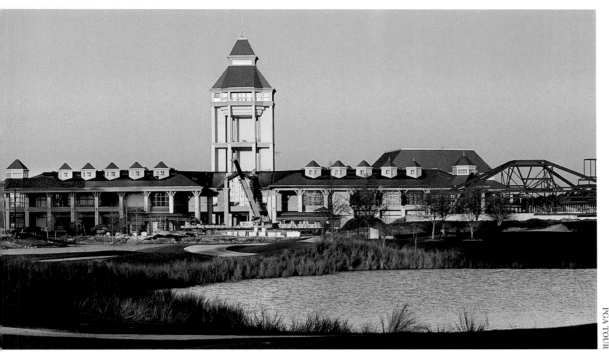

Construction at the new World Golf Hall of Fame began in 1995 and features a 75,000-square-foot museum. At right is the new IMAX theatre.

mitted and owned by Billy Dunavant and the Cummer Land Trust. Dunavant, the world's largest cotton merchant, had hired Jim Davidson, a former executive for the Arvida Corporation, to develop the property. In the early 1980s, Davidson worked with the TOUR in the development of the Valley Course at Sawgrass, and had stayed close with Beman and Kelly after moving across town. The Hall of Fame project and Saint Johns seemed like a perfect fit.

Dunavant donated 400 acres, 40 for the World Golf Village, including the Hall of Fame and a new building for PGA TOUR Productions, with the remainder for two 18-hole golf courses. Dunavant would get to keep 40 acres to develop with retail stores and a hotel.

Beman had talked the Fletcher brothers into the TPC at Sawgrass property for $1. Dunavant, who held the land since the 1970s, ended up giving the TOUR a better deal. "Vernon Kelly drove a hard bargain," said Beckwith. "He got the buck waived."

The pieces started coming together once Davidson convinced Dunavant that he would have to kick in $9 million to build the

I-95 interchange that would be the on-off ramps to International Golf Parkway. Soon after that, E. Verner Johnson and Associates was hired to design the museum building (they had done work at the Louvre and the Chicago Museum of Science and Industry), and Ralph Appelbaum, who designed several major museums in the United States, was commissioned to design the exhibitry.

The next step, and one of the biggest, was to get the state involved. In the late 1980s, the Florida Legislature had passed the Stadium Bill that would grant $2 million a year for 30 years to professional sports teams to move to the state. In return, these teams had to show an attendance level of 300,000 a year and generate at least $2 million a year in sales tax; in other words, not even counting the economic impact, it was a flat wash. Led by Kelly and Bowers — who knew how government worked — and backed by the support of local counties, chambers of commerce and legislatures, the TOUR lobbied hard in Tallahassee that the World Golf Village project should be considered for funds from the Stadium Bill.

The presentation was made in Tallahassee to six committees, so the story was told all over the legislature. In February of 1993, a reception was held at the Florida

Medical Association across the street from the State House. Gary Player, Chi Chi Rodriguez and Calvin Peete attended and by the time it came to a vote, on the last day of the session, support was so strong that the bill granting the $50 million passed by votes of 38-0 in the Senate and 102-2 in the House. The TOUR bonded the money, so they would have it all up front.

As this funding process was going on, Beman approached and sold LPGA Commissioner Charlie Mechem on the idea. He was now starting to realize how monumental to golf this could be if it became more than a PGA TOUR Hall of Fame, and the LPGA had just moved to a permanent headquarters just south of St. Augustine in Daytona Beach.

After Tim Finchem replaced Beman as Commissioner on June 1, 1994, he selected Beckwith as the Executive Director of the Hall of Fame. Then Finchem, with Beckwith's assistance, set out to recruit all of the other major golf organizations in the world to join the TOUR and the LPGA in the World Golf Village project.

The Royal and Ancient Golf Club of St. Andrews pledged its support and an exhibit exchange program was worked out. Shortly thereafter, the Augusta National Golf Club, the United States Golf Association, the National Golf Foundation and the Golf Course Superintendents of America joined the World Golf Foundation. The PGA of America ultimately decided to close Pinehurst and reassign the rights to the World Golf Hall of Fame. "That," said Beckwith, "completed the circle.

"Pulling together all of the organizations in golf was critical to the success of this project. You can't overestimate the importance of Tim Finchem's personal involvement or his personal commitment to the process," Beckwith said.

At this point the TOUR turned over $130 million in assets to the World Golf Foundation. A Board of Directors was established and the Hall of Fame Advisory Board first met in the fall of 1993. At one of the early meetings it was decided that rather than going back and revoting and reinducting, it would be better to move forward and grandfather in members of the existing LPGA Hall of Fame and World Golf Hall of Fame. The mission of the World Golf Foundation was to introduce golf to those who otherwise may not have an opportunity to experience the game, and through the golf experience promote scholastic

achievement, community service and the values of honesty, integrity and sportsmanship. Although not named at the time, this was the genesis of The First Tee Program.

"Without the PGA TOUR, and our commitment to this project, and our willingness to put a substantial amount of money at risk, this wouldn't have happened," Beman says. "When we turned over this project to the foundation, it was in excess of $130 million. Those are assets the TOUR could have had. But we made

the call that this could be bigger than our own dreams were at the beginning, and it could be more important to the game if we relinquished control. It was the right thing to do."

Kelly was steering the ship through its investor process. He visited with every hotel chain imaginable, but the only one developing its own properties was Hammons — and he wouldn't do the deal unless St. Johns County would put up the money for a convention center. His plan was this: the county puts up the money, and we'll pay back the county from revenues generated from different aspects of the project. It was a win-win for St. Johns, because it would bring more people to the area and result in more tourism for historic St. Augustine, but there were county commissioners who didn't see it that way. Although the convention center passed by a 4-3 vote, one commissioner formed a political action committee, which delayed the project with a lawsuit that took a full year before it was thrown out of court.

Construction didn't start until May 1996 because the Florida State Supreme Court did not rule on the suit until February of that year. "We've got newspaper articles saying we were due to open in 1995," Beckwith says. "Nobody knew we'd have these kinds of delays. It was '95, it was '96, it was '97."

Kelly brought Jim McGlothlin into the picture. McGlothlin owns The United Company, a fuel, oil and gas conglomerate that has a division called Scratch Golf Company of Hilton Head, S.C. Scratch Golf became the developers and operators of the three World Golf Village golf courses. McGlothlin is also an investor in the Vistana Resort at World Golf Village, a resort community of 400-plus one- and two-bedroom vacation ownership villas.

Now Kelly had something to sell. W.C. Bradley Co. and Cousins Properties ultimately would develop the upscale shopping and dining environment. EcoGroup of Naples, Fla., agreed to build The Residences at World Golf Village, a 31-acre community where senior executives of business and in-

THE FOUNDING PARTNER

Shell Oil Products Company's involvement in golf began in 1961, when it merged the finest players, the finest courses and the finest production staff to create the first made-for-television sports series, Shell's Wonderful World of Golf. The series has featured 92 matches in 58 countries, on courses like Pine Valley and St. Andrews, among players like Ben Hogan and Sam Snead, with scripts created by writers like Herbert Warren Wind. The series, which was reintroduced in 1994 and airs on ESPN, kicked off golf's explosion in the television age, and represents the company's ongoing association with the best that the sport has to offer.

Some 35 years later, the same commitment drew Shell to become the sole Founding Partner of the World Golf Village, the most ambitious project ever undertaken in golf. Located eight miles northwest of St. Augustine, Florida, along Interstate 95, World Golf Village will create an environment that not only honors the game of golf, its great players and its values and traditions, but also provides an entertaining and educational experience for golfers and non-golfers alike. The centerpiece is the World Golf Hall of Fame, the inductees of which this book honors.

As part of its 20-year agreement as Founding Partner, Shell will also play a leading role in the World Golf Foundation. The Foundation's mission, on behalf of the major golf organizations throughout the world, is to introduce young people to the game. Integral to this effort is "The First Tee" program, which will focus on building golf facilities in disadvantaged communities to allow youth, regardless of race or economic background, access to golf. Through the game's values, the First Tee will promote scholastic achievement, community service, integrity and a solid work ethic.

Since 1992, Shell's PGA TOUR event, the Shell Houston Open, has established itself as one of the leading children's charitable fundraising events in all of sports, giving more than $2.1 million to charity in 1997 alone. Shell also contributes to the growth of women's golf by being the 1998 "Official Gasoline of the Ladies Professional Golf Association."

AJGA

dustry will have access to a luxury condominium village with recreational amenities and state-of-the-art communications and information services.

The Mayo Clinic would establish a family care center to provide sports medicine and rehabilitation services, as well as physical examinations. IBM signed a 10-year agreement to design and integrate the World Golf Village's interactive information system.

It was all coming together, and then the Shell Oil Products Company stepped up and signed a 20-year contract to become Founding Partner of the World Golf Village. For more than 35 years, Shell had been recognized for its philanthropic endeavors and its development of the game of golf, and the mission of the World Golf Foundation was in line with that.

"There were plenty of opportunities to quit, to back off and say, 'To hell with this, let's not fool with this anymore, we've got better things to do," Beman said. "I just didn't want to do that. The promise of what it could be was worth the risks."

This new building at the World Golf Village houses the offices of PGA TOUR Productions as well as the offices for the World Golf Foundation.

"Those of us who believe in the values of golf want to see the opportunity to play the game extended to all segments of the population." — TIM FINCHEM

In November 1997, Tim Finchem held a news conference at the World Golf Village, then boarded a chartered jet and flew from St. Augustine Airport to New York, Detroit and Houston to announce The First Tee program. It was a little different view than when Beckwith flew over the old sand pit in 1995.

Finchem was joined by former President George Bush, who was named honorary chairman, Earl Woods and leaders within the golf community. "We want to create affordable entry points to golf for everyone who is interested in playing the game," Bush said.

Funds generated by the World Golf Hall of Fame would help do that—as would donations like the one the Arnold Palmer

The second golf course at the World Golf Village, named "The King and The Bear," is being designed by Arnold Palmer and Jack Nicklaus.

Golf Company made in March (15,000 sets of clubs, 3,000 bags). It will be a bandwagon that other corporations will surely mount as The First Tee gains momentum.

As Finchem flew around the country those two days, he was touched by the verve that people had for the concept of providing accessible golf for their communities. "I knew it would be powerful," Finchem said. "But I wasn't prepared for the enthusiasm that we ran into."

Since then, Finchem has focused on the idea that if golf can come together and build a World Golf Village, then that same coordination and common purpose could be used to push The First Tee program. Together, they could maximize the growth of the game and take golf to the masses.

As a symbol for the game, the World Golf Village has unlimited potential. It could be both the Disney World and the United Nations of golf.

"Bringing the entire world of golf together in one place, under one roof, is an accomplishment of which we can all be proud," Finchem said.

TEACHING AND CLUB PROFESSIONAL DIVISION

Tournament Sponsors Association

PGATTA

STTA

Patty Berg

No figure in women's golf spanned as many eras or did as much for her sport as Patty Berg.

Berg was all things to women's golf — a superb player, a great promoter, a wonderful teacher, a charismatic personality. And her gift has been measured over a long period of time. Berg won her first professional event in 1941, in the infancy of women's pro golf, and her last in 1962. But even after cancer surgery in 1971, Berg was still competing at the age of 62 in 1980. Hip replacement surgery later that year finally ended her competitive career.

In all, Berg won 57 times as a professional, including the first U.S. Women's Open in 1946 (the only time it was played at match play), the Western Open seven times, and Titleholders Championship four times. What made these totals even more remarkable is that for the entire prime of her professional career, Berg was competing while carrying a full schedule of exhibitions and clinics. She recently estimated that she had given more than 10,000 all over the world.

For Berg, golf was a high calling. One of her rules was: "Don't think you really win until you live up to that high thing within you that makes you do your best, no matter what."

Berg was born Feb. 13, 1918, in Minneapolis, Minnesota. Her father was a prosperous grain merchant, who belonged to the Interlachen C.C. Berg was an all-around athlete as a schoolgirl, competing in speed skating and even playing on a neighborhood football team that included future University of Oklahoma coach Bud Wilkinson. At 13, she turned her focus to golf, and has never stopped.

After a shaky introduction to amateur golf in the Minneapolis City Championship of 1933, Berg dedicated the next year to her game and won the event in 1934. "That was my proudest victory ever," she said. "After that, I began to dream."

In 1935, the Women's Amateur came to Interlachen, and Berg made it to the final where she was beaten, 3 and 2, by by Glenna Collet Vare. She lost the final again in 1937, but won the championship in 1938, a year in which she won 10 of the 13 amateur events she entered.

Berg turned professional in 1940, when there were only a handful of women professionals. Her income was earned doing clinics and exhibitions for Wilson Sporting Goods. For her first victory, the 1941 Women's Western Open, she received a $100 war bond.

Shortly after, Berg was in a car accident that left her left knee severely injured. The leg had to be reset twice, but during 18 months away from golf, Berg rehabilitated successfully by working out in the camp of a boxer. After a two-year stint in the Marines, in which she went to cadet school and graduated a second lieutenant, Berg won the first U.S. Women's Open in 1946, defeating Betty Jameson in Spokane, 5 and 4.

In 1948, the LPGA was established, and Berg, along with Babe Didrickson Zaharias, Betty Jameson and Louise Suggs, became the Big Four of the women's game. Berg, who was also the association's first president, won seven titles that first year. She was the LPGA's leading money winner in 1954, 1955, and 1957, won the Vare Trophy for lowest scoring average in 1953, 1955, and 1956, and was three times voted outstanding woman athlete of the year by the Associated Press. She is the first woman to win $100,000 in career earnings. In 1963, the USGA honored her with the Bob Jones Award.

Only 5-2, with red hair and a freckled face, Berg was known as a supreme shotmaker. Carol Mann called Berg "the most knowledgeable person, man or woman, of different golf shots that I've ever known." According to Mickey Wright, "Patty Berg is the consummate perfect golfer for a woman."

THE BERG RECORD

Major Championship Victories . . . 15
  U.S. Women's Open: 1946
  Western Open: 1941, 1943, 1948, 1951, 1955, 1957, 1958
  Titleholders: 1937, 1938, 1939, 1948, 1953, 1955, 1957

LPGA Tour Victories 57

Other Significant Victories
  Women's Amateur: 1938

Vare Trophy: 1953, 1955, 1956

Leading Money Winner: 1954, 1955, 1957

Bob Jones Award: 1963

Walter Hagen

Walter Hagen was golf's greatest showman, a flamboyant, princely romantic who captivated the public and his peers with sheer panache. He was "Sir Walter," and "The Haig." Such is his legacy as the most colorful character the game has ever seen that it often overshadows what a supreme player he was.

Hagen was the world's first full-time tournament professional. He won so often and in such lavish style that he single-handedly ushered the playing pro — who through the early century was clearly of a lower station than the game's wealthy amateurs — into the socially exclusive world of golf. As Arnold Palmer, the other great democrat of his sport, once said at a dinner honoring Hagen: "If not for you, Walter, this dinner tonight would be downstairs in the pro shop, not in the ballroom."

Of course, what gave weight to Hagen's personna was his often underrated talent and and never overrated champion's heart. Hagen won 11 professional major championships, second only to Jack Nicklaus's total of 18. Between 1914 and 1929, he won the PGA Championship five times (four of them in a row, the only time that has been accomplished in a major championship); the British Open four times, and the U.S. Open twice. He also won the Western Open five times between 1916 and 1932, when it was widely considered a major championship.

Hagen is generally considered the greatest match player of all time. He once won 22 straight 36-hole matches in the PGA and, between the first round in 1921 and the fourth round of 1928, 32 out of 33. With a long game often made erratic by the pronounced sway in his swing, but with an incredible ability to scramble and putt, Hagen lived by the principle that "three of *those* and one of *them* still count four." After he defeated Bob Jones 12 and 11 in a 72-hole challenge match in 1926 — which temporarily decided which of them was the greatest golfer of the

day — even the gentlemanly Jones couldn't contain his frustration. "When a man misses his drive, and then misses his second shot, and then wins the hole with a birdie," said Jones, "it gets my goat."

Hagen had a model attitude during competition, one part bravado and five parts serenity. He understood completely that the only shot that matters is the next one, and wouldn't let a bad one ruffle him. "I expect to make at least seven mistakes a round," he said. "Therefore, when I make a bad shot, it's just one of the seven." He never complained about bad breaks, and, perhaps because of that attitude, always seemed to be getting good ones. "I love to play with Walter," said Jones. "He can come nearer beating luck itself than anybody I know."

It was all a natural extension of his overall philosophy of life. Born in Rochester, N.Y., on Dec. 21, 1892, the son of a blacksmith, Hagen came from modest beginnings and entered golf as a caddy, but he resolved to live big. "I never wanted to be a millionaire," he said. "I just wanted to live like one." Although an imposing six feet tall, with slick black hair and covered in the finest fabrics, Hagen nonetheless had a kindly face and a twinkle of irony that invited rather than repelled the common man. His gestures were grand, but wonderfully human. When he won the 1922 British Open at Royal St. George's, Hagen's reaction to professionals not being allowed in the clubhouse was to hire an Austro-Daimler limousine, park it directly in front of the clubhouse, and change his clothes and take his meals in the car.

Hagen's once expressed his creed in these words: "You're only here for a short visit. Don't hurry. Don't worry. And be sure to smell the flowers along the way." When he died in Traverse City, Mich., on Oct. 5, 1969, there was no doubt he had lived it.

THE HAGEN RECORD

Major Championship Victories. . . . 11
  U.S. Open: 1914, 1919
  British Open: 1922, 1924, 1928, 1929
  PGA: 1921, 1924, 1925, 1926, 1927

PGA TOUR Victories 40

Ryder Cup Teams 6
  (7-1-1) 1927, 1929, 1931, 1933, 1935
  Captain: 1927, 1929, 1931, 1933, 1935, 1937

Ben Hogan

It was said Ben Hogan had the secret. He may or may not have—it was not the nature of the man to say. But if one player deserved to have it—by dint of total dedication and immersion in the game's mystery—it would be Ben Hogan.

Hogan had a code: Work, study, endure—that he never betrayed. The way he unwaveringly applied his code to achieving total control of the golf ball engendered a respect that surpasses that of any other player. When he won, it was completely deserved. When he lost, it was poignant, because no man ever gave so much. "I always outworked everybody," he said. "Work never bothered me like it bothers some people."

Hogan's record just happened to be something of a byproduct of this higher calling. He won 63 tournaments, his first in 1938 at the Hershey Four Ball (with Vic Ghezzi) and the last the 1959 Colonial. He won nine majors, and is one of only four men to win the Masters, the U.S. Open, the British Open and the PGA at least once. In 1953, he won all three majors he played in, missing the PGA because the dates conflicted with his only journey to the British Open.

Because he was the master of control, the U.S. Open was the canvas upon which Hogan did his best work. He won it four times, 1948, 1950, 1951 and 1953. From 1940 to 1960, excluding the championships of 1949 and 1957, both of which he missed due to injury, Hogan never finished out of the top 10 at any U.S. Open.

Hogan was born May 13, 1912 in Dublin, Texas. His father was a blacksmith who died when Ben was nine. After moving to Fort Worth, Hogan began his life in golf as a caddy, along with Byron Nelson, at the Glen Garden C.C. Hogan joined the professional circuit in 1932, and had very little early success. Small but strong at 5-7, 140 pounds, Hogan was a long hitter who was often undone by a hook. He went broke twice, and when he was on the verge a third time on the eve of the 1938 Oakland Open, he thought seriously about giving up. Instead, he shot a final-round 69 to finish second and win $380 to keep going. "I played harder that day than I ever played before or ever will again," he said.

Hogan didn't bloom until he found "a secret"— believed by some to be a weakening of his left hand along with the pronounced clockwise rotation of his left arm on the backswing — that allowed him to play a "power" fade. After several close calls in major championships, he won his first major at the 1946 PGA. When he won the 1948 PGA Championship in May and the U.S. Open at Riviera three weeks later, Hogan felt he was at his peak.

But on Feb. 2, 1949, a Greyhound bus crossed a center divider and crashed into the car carrying Hogan and his wife, Valerie. Hogan nearly died, and suffered permanent leg injuries. Miraculously, Hogan won the 1950 U.S. Open at Merion in 18-hole playoff with George Fazio and Lloyd Mangrum. "Merion meant the most," he would say later.

Even though Hogan only played a few tournaments a year thereafter, his best golf was ahead. In 1951, he won his first Masters and the U.S. Open at Oakland Hills. In 1953, he had his greatest year, winning his second Masters, his fourth U.S. Open, and his only British Open.

He played his last official event in 1971.

THE HOGAN RECORD

Major Championship Victories . . . 9
  Masters: 1951, 1953
  U.S. Open: 1948, 1950, 1951, 1953
  British Open: 1953
  PGA: 1946, 1948
PGA TOUR Victories 63
Ryder Cup Teams 4
  (3-0-0) 1947, 1951
  Captain 1947, 1949, 1967
PGA Player of the Year: 1948, 1950,
  1951, 1953
Vardon Trophy: 1940, 1941, 1948
Leading Money Winner: 1940, 1941,
  1942, 1946, 1948
Bob Jones Award: 1976

Robert Tyre Jones, Jr.

More than any player in history, Bobby Jones is the model of the complete golfer. Supremely gifted, Jones was also a man of vast intelligence and profound character, and he merged all three forces to become not only a singular champion, but a genuine hero. Wrote Herbert Warren Wind, "In the opinion of many people, of all the great athletes, Jones came the closest to being what we call a great man."

As a golfer, Jones was a giant. In the 1920s, he was "an ultra-athlete," according to writer and historian Charles Price, "recognized at being better at his game than any other athlete was at his." While there is no doubt Jones is the finest amateur golfer the game has ever produced, there's a strong argument that he was the greatest golfer, period. Beginning with his victory in the 1923 U.S. Open at Inwood, and ending with his U.S. Amateur victory at Merion in 1930, Jones won 13 championships in 20 tries, the most imposing run of major titles the game has ever seen.

His crowning glory was The Grand Slam of 1930, in which he became the only golfer ever to win U.S. Amateur, British Amateur, British Open and U.S. Open in the same year, indeed, the only golfer to win all four in a career. When he retired at the end of that year at the age of 28, *The New York Times* noted the occasion in an editorial that read, "With dignity, he quit the scene on which he nothing common did, or mean."

Jones was born on March 17, 1902, in Atlanta. He was clearly a prodigy, and his first championship was the 1916 U.S. Amateur, where as a 14-year-old he went to the third round.

From the beginning, Jones's swing possessed "a drowsy beauty," in the words of Bernard Darwin. Yet Jones was passionate man who had to overcome his own frailties of temperament. The strain of competition would cause him to lose as much as 18 pounds in a week. After winning the 1926 U.S. Open, he suddenly broke into tears in his Columbus, Ohio, hotel room, the strain catching up to him. He had to dominate a fiery temper that hindered him as a youth. As talented as he was, he did not win his first championship until 1923, prompting the early part of his career to be labeled "The Seven Lean Years." But Jones had a revelation when he discovered that the key to winning was learning to score well when playing badly. "I think this is what I learned to do best of all," wrote Jones, and "The Seven Fat Years" ensued.

Jones accomplished all this while playing competitive golf no more than three months in a year at any point in his life. The rest of the time was dedicated to academics, and later, the workaday world of the law. He studied mechanical engineering at Georgia Tech, graduating in three years, received a degree in English Literature from Harvard and attended law school at Emory University, withdrawing in his third semester to pass the bar. He would go on to become one of the game's most lucid and enlightening writers.

Besides his record and character, Jones's greatest legacy is the Augusta National Golf Club and the Masters Tournament, which he founded in 1934. He played in the tournament several times, never finishing better than 13th. In 1948, he developed syringomyelia, a fluid-filled cavity in his spinal cord causing first pain, then paralysis. Jones never played golf again, and was eventually restricted to a wheelchair until his death on Dec. 18, 1971.

As Wind wrote, "As a young man he was able to stand up to just about the best that life can offer, which isn't easy, and later he stood up with equal grace to just about the worst."

The USGA's award for distinguished sportsmanship is the Bob Jones Award. "What Jones did was create a model that everyone, consciously or unconsciously, followed," said William Campbell, "It is why we have so many fine people in golf. He showed the world how to do it."

THE JONES RECORD

Major Championship Victories . . . 13
  U.S. Amateur: 1924, 1925, 1927, 1928, 1930
  British Amateur: 1930
  U.S. Open: 1923, 1926, 1929, 1930
  British Open: 1926, 1927, 1930
Walker Cup Teams 5
  (9-1-0) 1922, 1924, 1926, 1928, 1930
  Captain 1928, 1930
Founded Augusta National Golf Club: 1933
Captain, World Amateur Team Championship: 1958

Byron Nelson

Just as there is no argument that perfection in golf is unattainable, no one argues that Byron Nelson has come the closest to attaining it.

Nelson's streak of 11 victories in a row in 1945 is considered the least attainable record not only in golf, but in sports. His total of 18 victories that year, seven second-place finishes, his 19 consecutive rounds under 70, and his scoring average of 68.33 (and 67.45 in the fourth round), sets the standard for the greatest single season in the history of the game.

Nelson is the player most often compared to a machine. In fact, when the USGA developed a mechanical device for testing golf balls and clubs, it named it "Iron Byron." Nelson is also a kind man of quiet dignity for whom the nickname, Lord Byron, also fit just as well.

"As a competitor, Byron was able to be mean and tough and intimidating — and pleasant," said Ken Venturi, whom Nelson mentored. "You can always argue who was the greatest player, but Byron is the finest gentleman the game has ever known."

In a relatively brief career, Nelson won 54 sanctioned tournaments, including the Masters in 1937 and 1942, the U.S. Open in 1939 and the PGA Championship in 1940 and 1945. In the 40s, he finished in the money 113 straight times. He retired from full-time competition in 1946.

Nelson was born Feb. 4, 1912, outside Waxahachie, Texas, the son of a cotton farmer. He and a boy from the other side of Fort Worth, Ben Hogan, both caddied at the Glen Garden C.C., where young Byron defeated Ben in a playoff for the caddy championship in 1927. Nelson turned pro in 1932.

Tall and rangy at 6-1 with enormous hands, Nelson achieved the pinnacle by developing an action that is considered the basis for the modern golf swing. Coming of age just as the steel shaft was replacing hickory, Nelson learned that using the big muscles in the hips and legs could be a more reliable, powerful and effective way to hit a golf ball than the more wristy method that had been employed in the era of hickory. Nelson was particularly noteworthy for the way his swing was more upright and along the target line, employing a full shoulder turn with restricted wrist cock, and for the way he kept his knees flexed in the downswing.

When Nelson was developing his swing, he would sometimes be stricken with episodes of shanking, until he found a forward swing correction. "I actually felt like I moved my head back while my body went forward," he said. "The more I did that, the better I got." Nelson also believed one of the keys to his ability was an uncanny sense for judging distance.

Nelson reached his peak as World War II was ending. In 75 starts from 1944 to the end of 1946, he won 34 times, and finished second 16 times. In those three years, he finished out of the top 10 just once, with a tie for 13th at Pensacola in 1946. Arnold Palmer, who grew up with Nelson as his idol, said, "Byron Nelson accomplished things on the pro Tour that never have been and never will be approached."

Nelson retired from full time competition after that 1946 season, settling down at 34 to a Texas ranch whose purchase had been a large part of his motivation when he was winning so often. His last official victory was the 1951 Bing Crosby Pro-Am, and he won the 1955 French Open. Along with his influence on Venturi, Nelson helped many young players with their games, including Tom Watson. Nelson also worked for several years as a television commentator for ABC Sports.

THE NELSON RECORD

Major Championship Victories 5
  Masters: 1937, 1942
  U.S. Open: 1939
  PGA: 1940, 1945
PGA TOUR Victories 54
Ryder Cup Teams 3
  (3-1-0) 1937, 1947
  Captain 1965
Vardon Trophy: 1939
Leading Money Winner: 1944, 1945
PGA TOUR Record: 18 wins and
  11 consecutive wins in 1945

Jack Nicklaus

By the most objective measure of all—the record—Jack Nicklaus is the greatest player who ever lived.

There was an immensity to Nicklaus's game. Nicklaus combined tremendous physical ability with boundless mental and psychological resources. At those times when his game was in full song, he would dominate his competition. But Nicklaus's ultimate genius was that when it wasn't, he often found a way to win because he would almost never beat himself. His style was a combination of explosive shotmaking and conservative management that calculated all factors—the course, his opponents and how he was playing. As a golfer, Nicklaus was both Secretariat and Einstein.

Subjective assessments, however, are secondary, because Nicklaus's record is a colossus that encapsulates the game. In sheer numbers, it is awesome.

Between 1962 and 1986, Nicklaus won 70 official events on the PGA TOUR, second in total only to Sam Snead. But it is Nicklaus's performance in major championships alone sets him above all others. He won 20—two U.S. Amateurs, a record six Masters, a record-tying four U.S. Opens, three British Opens and a record-tying five PGAs. He completed three full cycles of the modern Grand Slam, something no other player has done more than once. If performance in major championships is the ultimate criterion, than no golfer has ever set himself apart like Nicklaus.

Nicklaus was born Jan. 21, 1940, in Columbus, Ohio. His father, Charlie, was a pharmacist who introduced his son to sports and remained his greatest friend and supporter. While growing up at the Scioto C.C. under the tutelage of Jack Grout, Nicklaus came to idolize Bobby Jones, whose 13 major championships became the reference point for his own career.

As an amateur, Nicklaus was clearly a prodigy.

He won the 1956 Ohio State Open at age 16. Three years later, he defeated Charlie Coe, 1 up, in an epic final in the U.S. Amateur, and won it again at Pebble Beach in 1961. In between, he tied for second at the 1960 U.S. Open and shot an astounding 269 at Merion in the World Amateur Team Championship.

By the time Nicklaus came on the pro scene in 1962, he was a stout, crew-cut dynamo of 215 pounds who was about to change the game. With a mighty upright swing that allowed him to hit the ball high and generally with a slight fade, Nicklaus became the longest controlled driver in the game's history, as well as the most devastating long-iron player. His technique and strength also allowed him to escape from high grass with more power and control than his rivals. Along with a reliable putting touch that was particularly consistent inside of six feet, Nicklaus's arsenal was designed to conquer the narrow fairways, deep rough and firm, fast greens that characterize major championships. By 1967, he had won seven of them. Between 1970 and 1975, leaner and more fashionably coiffed, he won seven more.

On the PGA TOUR, Nicklaus led the money list eight times, twice while playing only 16 events.

Between 1962 and 1979, he finished in the top ten in 243 of the 357 official events he played in, a rate of 68 percent.

For all his physical gifts, it was Nicklaus's ability to concentrate and gather himself for decisive moments that most separated him. This was never more evident than in his most fulfilling triumph, the 1986 Masters, where, at the age of 46, Nicklaus put together a final-round 65 that included a 30 on the back nine to win by one.

Through it all, Nicklaus completed the ultimate champion's profile by being a gracious loser. He finished second 19 times in majors, but always gave credit to the winner. Win or lose, Jack Nicklaus was the greatest.

THE NICKLAUS RECORD

Major Championship Victories . . . 20
  U.S. Amateur: 1959, 1961
  U.S. Open: 1962, 1967, 1972, 1980
  Masters: 1963, 1965, 1966, 1972,
      1975, 1986
  British Open: 1966, 1970, 1978
  PGA: 1963, 1971, 1973, 1975, 1980
Walker Cup Teams 2
  (4-0-0) 1959, 1961
PGA TOUR Victories 70
SENIOR PGA TOUR Victories . . 10
Ryder Cup Teams 8
  (17-8-3) 1969, 1971, 1973,
            1975, 1977, 1981
  Captain 1983, 1987
PGA Player of the Year: 1964, 1965,
    1967, 1971, 1972, 1973, 1975, 1976
Leading Money Winner: 1964, 1965,
    1967, 1971, 1972, 1973, 1975, 1976

Francis Ouimet

They were the shots heard 'round the world,' and they too started a revolution.

At the 1913 U.S. Open at The Country Club, Francis Ouimet, a 20 year old former caddie, didn't just beat British legends Harry Vardon and Ted Ray, he changed the perceptions of an entire sport. Ouimet's stunning triumph captured the imagination of sports fans across the globe, sweeping away the notion that golf was a stuffy game for the old and rich. Ouimet was American golf's first great hero, and he remains one of the most beloved figures in the sport's history.

Ouimet seemed to step from the pages of a Dickens novel. He had grown up across the street from The Country Club in a working-class home and learned the game with the one old club his older brother, Wilfred, had procured as a caddie. The two boys built three makeshift holes in the family backyard, incorporating a gravel pit, a swamp, a brook and a patch of long, rough grass. Sunken tomato cans were used as cups. At 11, Ouimet began caddying at The Country Club, and by his late teens, he had begun to make a name for himself in tournament competition. After winning the 1913 Massachusetts State Amateur Championship, Ouimet was inspired to enter the National Open.

After three rounds he somehow found himself tied with Vardon, a four-time winner of the British Open, and the reigning British Open champ Ray, whose walrus mustache and length off the tee were equally outsized. During the tense final round both Englishmen stumbled home with 79s, and, after a jittery 43 on the front nine, Ouimet joined their playoff by birdieing the 71st hole.

The following day, all three men went out in 38, and Ouimet took his first lead when Vardon and Ray both three-putted the par-3 10th. By the par-4 17th Ray had given up the fight but Vardon was only one behind when he caught a bunker with his drive and took bogey. Ouimet then drilled a 15-foot birdie putt to put championship on ice and endear himself to the world, with a little bit of help from his ten-year-old caddie Eddie Lowery, a pint-sized neighborhood kid who added a touch of whimsy to the photographs.

Ouimet proved he was no fluke by winning the 1914 U.S. Amateur, but he when he subsequently opened a sporting goods shop he was banned from amateur competition by the USGA, a miscarriage of justice that was later reversed. Ouimet returned to play on the inaugural Walker Cup team in 1921 and the 14 that followed. In 1931, temples specked with gray, he won another U.S. Amateur at the age of 38. Ouimet was an important international figure as well. In 1951, he became the first American to captain the Royal and Ancient Golf Club in St. Andrews.

His legacy transcends tournament victories. In 1913 it is estimated only 350,000 Americans played golf. Ten years later, fueled by Ouimet's heroics, that number was up to 2,000,000. So it is that Ouimet is rightfully called the Father of American Golf. In 1963, the U.S. Open was again held at The Country Club to commemmorate the 50th anniversary of his victory. Said Ouimet in 1932, "To me, the ground here is hallowed. The grass grows greener, the trees bloom better, there is even a warmth to the rocks. Somehow or other the sun seems to shine brighter on The Country Club than any other place that I have ever known." He died in nearby Newton in 1967.

THE OUIMET RECORD

Major Championship Victories 3
  U.S. Open: 1913
  U.S. Amateur: 1914, 1931

Walker Cup Teams 8
  (9-5-2) 1922, 1923, 1924,
      1926, 1928, 1930, 1932, 1934
  Captain 1932, 1934

Bob Jones Award: 1955

Arnold Palmer

No figure in the history of golf has injected more excitement into the game over a sustained period than Arnold Palmer. Palmer's ability to win with boldness and charisma was the single biggest factor in the game's explosive growth after 1960. For people born in the second half of the 20th century, it was as if Arnold Palmer invented golf.

Hyperbole aside, Palmer brought golf to the masses. The open passion with which he played, from his whirlybird followthrough on the tee to his fierce animation on the greens, was different from the cool intensity that the great players before him had cultivated. Palmer lashed at the ball with all his might and charged his putts recklessly. With his thick forearms and wasp waist, he was a sweaty, 5-10, 165-pound blue collar dynamo who joyfully made golf an athletic event - the perfect figure to usher in golf's television era. "Arnold Palmer did not play golf, we thought," wrote Dan Jenkins. "He nailed up beams, reupholstered sofas, repaired air conditioning units. He was the most immeasurable of all golf champions."

As telegenic as Palmer was, he was most magnetic as the leader of the throng that called themselves Arnie's Army. "I tried to look the whole gallery in the eye," he said. "Some people think of me as just plain lucky, and I can't argue with them," he once said. "I would like to say, however, that a man might be walking around lucky and not know it unless he tries."

Nobody tried like Palmer. He learned to love the game in Latrobe, Pa., where he was born on Sept. 10, 1929. His father, Deacon, was the professional, at the nine-hole Latrobe C.C., and the Palmer's lived on the golf course. Young Arnold dreamed of playing golf for a living, and after he won the U.S. Amateur in 1954 — the victory that remains his favorite — he began living his dream.

Between 1955 and 1973, Palmer won 63 PGA TOUR events including seven professional major championships — the Masters in 1958, 1960, 1962 and 1964, the 1960 U.S. Open, and the 1961 and 1962 British Opens. His most most magical golf was produced in 1960, a year he won eight official events. At the Masters, he birdied the final two holes to edge Ken Venturi by one. Two months later at the U.S. Open at Cherry Hills, he began the final round on Saturday seven strokes and 14 players behind. But he drove the green on the 340-yard first hole, shot 30 on the front nine, and finished with a 65 to win by two. The Palmer "charge" was born, and for the next two years, he seemed unbeatable down the stretch. The next month, when Palmer made a pilgrimage to St. Andrews for the British Open, his presence singlehandedly elevated the game's oldest championship from disrepair to its rightful place.

With a muscular swing that produced a piercing draw, Palmer was one of the finest drivers of the ball who ever lived, and from a distinctive pigeon-toed stance, a superb putter. He lead the PGA TOUR's money list four times, and in 1963 became the first player to win more than $100,000 in a season. He played on six Ryder Cups teams, and was the winning captain twice.

Palmer's defeats were as dramatic as his victories. In 1961, he lost the Masters by one stroke when he double bogeyed the 72nd hole. He lost playoffs in three U.S. Opens, the first to Jack Nicklaus in 1962; the second to Julius Boros in 1963; and the third and most heartbreaking to Billy Casper at The Olympic Club in 1966, where Palmer had led by seven strokes with nine holes to play in regulation. Palmer's best finish in the PGA Championship was second — three times — which kept him from attaining the career Grand Slam.

But his losses, like everything Palmer did, only served to further endear him to his legions. For more than four decades under the spotlight, Arnold Palmer signed every autograph, shook every hand, and most of all, gave everything to every shot.

THE PALMER RECORD

Major Championship Victories . . . 8
  U.S. Amateur: 1955
  Masters: 1958, 1960, 1964, 1966
  U.S. Open: 1960
  British Open: 1961, 1962
PGA TOUR Victories 60
SENIOR PGA TOUR Victories . . 10
Ryder Cup Teams 7
  (22-8-2) 1961, 1963, 1965,
        1967, 1971, 1973
    Captain 1963, 1975
Vardon Trophy: 1961, 1962, 1964, 1967
Leading Money Winner: 1958, 1960,
        1962, 1963
PGA Player of the Year: 1960, 1962

Gary Player

When speaking of Gary Player, its common for observers to say something along the lines of, "He's done more with less than any golfer I've ever seen."

The less is Player's improbable 5-7, 160 pounds, his unorthodox method, his hailing from a small country in a remote corner of the world. The more includes nine major championships, the modern Grand Slam, 161 tournament victories around the world – including 21 official PGA TOUR victories – and a symmetrical nine SENIOR TOUR majors. Yet Player, in his forthright way, differs with a reductionist view of his career. "I had a great deal of talent," he will say, before adding, "But talent alone will only take you so far."

No, with Player, there has always been a palpable sense of something extra. Perhaps no golfer has ever craved victory so much for such a long time. "What I have learned about myself," he wrote in his 1991 autobiography, "is that I am animal when it comes to achievement and wanting success. There is never enough success for me."

His peers, who included Arnold Palmer and Jack Nicklaus in their primes, knew it. "I don't think Gary was a great driver of the golf ball," said Nicklaus. "I don't think he was a great iron player. He was a good putter, not a great putter. But when he really needed to be, he was a great driver, and great iron player, and he made the putt when he needed to make it. Gary, as much as anyone I ever saw, has that thing inside him that champions have."

Gary Jim Player was born on Nov. 1, 1935, in Johannesburg, South Africa, the third of three children to Harry and Muriel Player. His father was a captain in a gold mine who spent most of his working life 12,000 feet underground. His mother was a well-educated woman who died of cancer when Gary was eight. Player wrote that her loss "has been a means for me, as it were, to settle some unfathomable debt."

He chose to try to pay it back as a golfer, although he didn't take up the game until he was 14.

He turned professional in 1953, at age 18, and quickly won several times in Africa, Europe and Australia. In 1957, he came to America, and upon seeing how far the game's best professionals hit the ball, intensified his exercise regimen, weakened his hooker's grip and set about learning how to carry the ball farther. The next year he won the Kentucky Derby Open, and was heartened by a second-place finish at the U.S. Open, where his idol, Ben Hogan, locked him with a stare and said, "Son, you are going to be a great player."

From there, Player was off. In his trademark all black outfits (inspired by his lifelong love of westerns) with body trim and biceps bulging from a weight-lifting program and high-fiber diet that were both 30 years ahead of their time — and with a bunker game that is considered the greatest ever developed — he willed himself to victory. He won the 1959 British Open at Muirfield for his first major, made the 1961 Masters his second, and the 1962 PGA at Aronimink his third. At the 1965 U.S. Open at Bellerive, Player defeated Kel Nagle in an 18-hole playoff to complete the modern Grand Slam by age 29.

His other majors include the 1972 PGA Championship, the 1968 and 1974 British Opens, and the 1974 and 1978 Masters. The last is perhaps Player's proudest victory, for he began the final round seven strokes out of the lead. But at age 42, he birdied seven of the final 10 holes to shoot 64 and win by a stroke.

Player is indisputably the greatest international golfer of all time. He estimates he has spent more than three years of his life in airplanes and travelled some 10 million miles. In every year from 1955 to 1982, Player won at least one sanctioned international tournament, a 27-year streak that is 10 years longer than anyone else has ever achieved. He won the World Match Play title five times, the Australian Open seven times, the South African Open 13 times. In winning the 1974 Brazilian Open, he shot the only 59 ever in a national open.

THE PLAYER RECORD

Major Championships Victories . . . 9
  U.S. Open: 1965
  Masters: 1961, 1974, 1978
  British Open: 1959, 1968, 1974
  PGA Championship: 1962, 1972
Total Tournaments Won 161
PGA TOUR Victories 21
SENIOR PGA TOUR Victories . . 21
Leading Money Winner: 1961

Gene Sarazen

As a competitor and innovator, Gene Sarazen spans golf history like no other great American player. From pugnacious whiz kid to equipment innovator to mature champion to senior statesman, Sarazen remains a presence well into his 90s. When he's not hitting the opening drive at the Masters each year, his ageless wit is a living bridge to the memories of Vardon, Hagen and Jones.

He was born Eugenio Saraceni, the son of an Italian carpenter from Rome, on Feb. 27, 1902 in Harrison, N.Y. He dropped out of school in sixth grade, and turned pro at age 16. It was then that he changed his name to Sarazen, because, he once said, "it sounded like a golfer."

At 5-5, 145 pounds, Sarazen was the shortest of golf's greatest champions. But he was solidly built and possessed a tremendous competitive heart. In 1922, at the age of 20, he arrived at the Skokie C.C. for his first U.S. Open and won, birdieing the final hole and becoming, with a closing 68, the first player to shoot under 70 in the final round to win. Later in the year, he won the PGA Championship at Oakmont. He then challenged Walter Hagen to a 72-hole *mano a mano* for the "world championship" and beat history's greatest match player. In 1932, he won both the British Open at Sandwich and the U.S. Open at Fresh Meadow, where he played the last 28 holes in 100 strokes, posting a closing round of 66 that would be a record for a winner until 1960.

"When Sarazen saw a chance at the bacon hanging over the last green," wrote his friend, Bob Jones, "he could put as much fire and fury into a finishing round as Jack Dempsey could put into a fight."

In 1934, Sarazen became became the first player to win the modern Grand Slam by capturing the 1935 Masters. In the final round of that tournament, he hit the most famous shot ever in major championship golf, holing a 4-wood from 235 yards away for a double-eagle 2 on the 15th hole that tied him with Craig Wood, whom he defeated the next day in a playoff. The "shot heard round the world" helped put the Masters on the map.

Altogether, Sarazen won seven major championships among his 36 victories around the world, and as late as 1940 nearly won his third U.S. Open, losing to Lawson Little in a playoff. He was known for his compact but ferocious swing, the grim delight he seemed to take from competition and his fast play. In 1947, he and George Fazio played a round at the Augusta National in one hour and 57 minutes.

But as great as Sarazen's playing record, he did as much for the game with his innovative nature. Taking a tip from Ty Cobb, he developed a weighted practice club in 1929. In 1931, while being taught by Howard Hughes how to fly a plane, Sarazen noticed the tail adjusting downward during take off and came upon the idea for the modern sand wedge, which he spent months perfecting. He later called it his biggest contribution to golf. Later, he lobbied unsuccessfully to have the hole enlarged from 4 1/4 inches in diameter to eight inches.

Sarazen was perhaps the greatest early ambassador of golf among American pros, playing exhibitions all over the world. He earned his nickname, "The Squire," after he bought a farm for his family in upstate New York. In the early 60s, he came back into the public eye as the host of *Shell's Wonderful World of Golf*.

In 1973, on the 50th anniversary of his first appearance in the British Open, the 71 year old Sarazen made a hole-in-one with a punched 5-iron at the short par-3 eighth hole, known as the Postage Stamp, at Troon. In 1992, he was presented the Bob Jones Award from the United States Golf Association. He lives in Marco Island, Fla.

THE SARAZEN RECORD

Major Championship Victories . . . 7
  Masters: 1935
  U.S. Open: 1922, 1932
  British Open: 1932
  PGA: 1922, 1923, 1933
PGA TOUR Victories 36
Ryder Cup Teams 6
  (7-2-3) . . 1927, 1929, 1931, 1933, 1935, 1937

Sam Snead

Sam Snead was the greatest athlete among golf's great champions. The swing he employed to win tournaments over six decades remains the archetype of power and grace, his longevity the benchmark of an incredible talent.

In more than 50 years as an active competitor, Snead won a record 81 official PGA TOUR victories, and he can safely claim more than 140 worldwide. Nicknamed "The Slammer" for the strength of his shots, he won seven major championships.

At a long-limbed 5-10 and 185 pounds, Snead was classically configured and preternaturally gifted. In high school, he could run the 100-yard dash in 10 seconds flat. Into his 70s he could, from a dead standstill, kick the top of a seven-foot doorway. His movements were almost musical, and it was no surprise to anyone that Snead had taught himself to play the banjo and the trumpet by ear. As a boy who preferred to go barefoot, he learned golf in much the same way, and on those rare occasions when his rhythm was off, he could regain it by removing his shoes and socks, as he did for nine holes at the 1942 Masters. Once during a discussion of his swing keys, Snead said simply, "I try to feel oily." On another occasion he said, "When I swing at a golf ball right, my mind is blank and my body is loose as a goose."

Samuel Jackson Snead was born May 27, 1912, in Ashwood, Va., the youngest of five brothers. At the time, his mother, Laura, was 47. Golf first captivated him while watching his older brother, Homer, belt balls across the family's cow and chicken farm, and soon he was fashioning his own clubs out of swamp maple limbs and using balls he had found caddying at the nearby Homestead Hotel Golf Course in Hot Springs. He got his first assistant pro job at 19 at The Homestead, moved to the Greenbrier in 1935 as the playing professional, and in 1936, joined the PGA TOUR.

Immensely long off the tee and a creative shotmaker, Snead took the TOUR by storm. He won four times in 1937, and eight times in 1938. Under the guidance of promoter Fred Corcoran, who marketed Snead as a hillbilly force of nature out of the Back Creek Mountains of Virginia, he quickly became golf's prime attraction. "Sam Snead," said Gene Sarazen, "is the only person who came into the game possessing every physical attribute—a sound swing, power, a sturdy physique, and no bad habits."

The next year, he was even hotter, but suffered a major setback at the U.S. Open at Spring Mill in Philadelphia. Thinking he needed a birdie on the 72nd hole to win, but in reality needing only a par-5, Snead made an eight to finish tied for fifth. He would go on to finish second in the U.S. Open four times, once when he missed a 30-inch putt on the final green of a playoff with Lew Worsham in 1947.

Still, Snead won three Masters, three PGAs and the British Open in 1946 at St. Andrews. He led the money list three times, won the Vardon Trophy four times, and played on seven Ryder Cup teams. His final major championship victory was perhaps his most memorable. At the 1954 Masters, Snead, tied after 72 holes with Ben Hogan, defeated him in an 18 hole playoff, 70 to 71.

Short putting eventually stopped Snead from winning at his normal pace. Still, his achievements in his later years were remarkable. In 1965, Snead, at 52 years and 10 months, became the oldest winner of a PGA TOUR event when he won the Greater Greensboro Open for the eighth time. He was fourth in the PGA Championship at age 60 in 1972, and third in 1974 at age 62. "Desire is the most important thing in sport," he once said. "I have it. Jeez, no one has more than I've got."

THE SNEAD RECORD

Major Championship Victories . . . 7
  Masters: 1949, 1952, 1954
  British Open: 1946
  PGA: 1942, 1949, 1951

PGA TOUR Victories 81

SENIOR PGA TOUR Victories. . . 6

Other Significant Victories
  Greater Greensboro Open: 8 times
  PGA Seniors: 6 times
  World Seniors Championship: 5 times

Ryder Cup Teams 8
  (10-2-1) . 1937, 1947, 1949, 1951,
        1953, 1955, 1959
  Captain 1951, 1959, 1969

Vardon Trophy: 1938, 1949, 1950, 1955

Leading Money Winner: 1938, 1949, 1950

Harry Vardon

Harry Vardon was possessed with a talent and method so singular he was considered a shotmaking machine in the improvisational era of hickory and gutta percha. The winner of the British Open a record six times, he was golf's first superstar.

Vardon was a true original. On his own, he developed the Vardon Grip, in which the little finger of the right hand is rested on top of the index finger of the left hand, the grip used by 90 percent of good players today. Wrote Bernard Darwin of Vardon, "I do not think anyone who saw him play in his prime will disagree as to this, that a greater genius is inconceivable."

Vardon was born May 9, 1870, in Grouville, Jersey, one of the Channel Islands between England and France. The son of a gardener, he was one of six boys and two girls. When the town went about building a golf course, the children built their own, and Vardon taught himself the effortless, upright swing that would serve him the rest of his life.

Still, as a child he played very few actual rounds of golf, never had a lesson, and at age 13, became an apprentice gardener. He played in a few tournaments into his late teens, and didn't decide to make it a career until he saw that his older brother, Tom, had turned professional and was doing well in tournaments.

But Vardon was made for golf. Although only 5'9 1/2", and 155 pounds, he had enormous hands that melded perfectly around a club. He also possessed a sweet, peaceful temperament.

Most of all, Vardon had a swing that repeated monotonously. His swing was more upright and his ball flight higher than his contemporaries, giving Vardon's approach shots the advantage of greater carry and softer landing. He took only the thinnest of divots.

Vardon played in knickers (the first professional to do so), fancy-topped stockings, a hard collar and tie, and tightly buttoned jacket, but still there was a wonderful freedom to his movement. He allowed his left arm to bend as he reached the top of the backswing, and there was a lack of muscular stress or tension at any part of the swing. "Relaxation," he said, "added to a few necessary fundamental principles, is the basis of this great game."

Vardon won the British Open in 1896, 1898, 1899, 1903, 1911 and, at the age of 44, in 1914. He was second on four other occasions.

In 1900, Vardon toured America for the first time, playing some 88 matches, usually against the better ball of two opponents, winning 75 of them. Everywhere he went, he left a standard that within 20 years would propel Americans to world leadership in golf. Before leaving, he won the U.S. Open at the Chicago Golf Club.

Golf was never again so easy for Vardon. He felt that fashioning shots to American turf conditions got him into some bad habits, and the wound rubber Haskell ball that came into fashion reduced his shotmaking advantage over the field. Finally, after winning the British Open again in 1903, Vardon was diagnosed with tuberculosis. It forced him out of competition and into sanitariums for long spells until 1910.

Healed but enfeebled, Vardon validated his true greatness after the age of 40, winning the British Open again in 1911 and also, at the age of 44, in 1914. The previous year, Vardon had been beaten in a three way playoff for the U.S. Open at Brookline by Francis Ouimet. In 1920, at the age of 50, he led the U.S. Open by four strokes with only seven holes to play, before bad weather and a shaky putter left him in a tie for second.

Vardon died on March 20, 1937, in London. On both the European and U.S. PGA TOURS, the Vardon Trophy is awarded annually to the professional with the lowest stroke average.

THE VARDON RECORD

Major Championship Victories . . . 7
U.S. Open: 1900
British Open: 1896, 1898, 1899, 1903, 1911, 1914
Total Tournament Victories 62

Babe Didrikson Zaharias

Olympic gold medal winner in track and field. All-America basketball player in college. Champion golfer. If there was a Jim Thorpe among women athletes, it was Mildred "Babe" Didrikson Zaharias. As a golfer, she won 31 tournaments, including three U.S. Women's Opens, and helped found the Ladies Professional Golf Association. "Babe changed the game of golf for women," said Patty Berg.

Didrikson didn't even take up golf seriously until she was 21 years old. She was introduced to the game by Grantland Rice in Los Angeles during the 1932 Olympics. Somewhere in between winning gold medals in the javelin and hurdles — she might have won the high jump, too, had she not been disqualified — Didrikson joined Rice and three other sportswriters for a round of golf at Brentwood C.C. According to Rice, the Babe shot 91 that day and regularly hit drives measuring 250 yards.

The following year, while she was touring the country with the House of David baseball tours, Didrikson traveled back to Los Angeles and took golf lessons from pro Stan Kertes at Brentwood. Two years later, she won the Texas Women's Amateur Championship with an eagle on the 34th hole. The United States Golf Association ruled the following day that as a professional athlete, Didrikson could no longer compete in amateur golf events.

This led Didrikson to go on exhibition tours and celebrity pro-ams. In 1938, during a tournament in California, she was paired with a professional wrestler named George Zaharias. They married later that year, and with Zaharias supporting his

wife and managing her career, the Babe applied for amateur reinstatement. The USGA granted her wish in 1943, and immediately after World War II, Zaharias went on a tear that included the U.S. Women's Amateur in 1946 and the British Women's Amateur in 1947. Published reports had her winning 16 consecutive tournaments, and this led her to turn professional, sign with sports promoter Fred Corcoran and, along with Berg, help form the LPGA Tour.

As a professional, Zaharias was just as dominant, winning 31 of the 128 events she played from 1948-1953. Asked what the secret of her success was, Zaharias would usually answer with her favorite expression. "Aw," she'd say, "I just loosen my girdle and take a whack at it."

Zaharias's last seven wins, including the 1954 Women's Open, came after she was diagnosed for cancer and had a colostomy. That Women's Open victory, by 12 strokes over Betty Hicks at Salem (Mass.) C.C. was one of five victories that year. The pain returned in 1955, and although she won twice that year, it wasn't long before Babe Zaharias was gone. She died on Sept. 27, 1956, at the age of 42.

Berg called her "the most physically talented woman I've ever seen," and that statement applied not only to golf, but to the rest of the sports Babe Didrikson Zaharias mastered. These included bowling, tennis, and if card games count, those too. In her autobiography, *This Life I've Led*, Zaharias wrote, "All my life, I've had the urge to do things better than anyone else." She may have been the greatest woman athlete in history.

THE ZAHARIAS RECORD

Major Championship Victories . . . 12
  U.S. Women's Amateur: 1946
  British Women's Amateur: 1947
  Western Open: 1944, 1945, 1947, 1950
  U.S. Women's Open: 1948, 1950, 1954
  Titleholders: 1948, 1950, 1954
Vare Trophy: 1954
Leading Money Winner: 1948, 1949, 1950, 1951
Bob Jones Award: 1957
Associated Press Woman of the Year: 1931, 1945, 1946, 1947, 1950, 1954

Betty Jameson

A pioneer of woman's professional golf, Betty Jameson is one of only six women to have won both the U.S. Women's Open and U.S. Women's Amateur championships.

In her prime, Jameson was a tall, stylish woman who is sometimes referred to as golf's first "glamour girl." She was a founding member of both the Women's Professional Golf Association and the Ladies Professional Golf Association. She was also the first woman to break 300 for a 72-hole event.

Elizabeth Jameson was born May 19, 1919, in Norman, Okla. After her family moved to Dallas, she began playing golf at age 11 and was soon completing as many as 50 holes a day on a nine-hole course.

Her long, graceful swing was much admired. Herbert Warren Wind wrote after watching her that "all you are conscious of is how perfectly the left hand does what the left hand is supposed to do, and, as she moves into the ball, an acceleration which keeps building so smoothly that it is hardly perceptible." According to Lawson Little, Jameson had "the soundest swing, the best pivot and the greatest follow through of the hips, of any woman player except Joyce Wethered."

Jameson won the 1932 Texas Publinx at age 13, followed by the state championship. At age 15, she captured the Southern Amateur and went to win it four years in a row. In 1939, she won the U.S. Amateur at Wee Burn in Connecticut, and repeated the next year at Pebble Beach. In 1942, she became first player to win the Western Open and the Western Amateur in the same year.

Something went out of Jameson when her mother died in 1942. "My mother knew I could be a world beater — that was the old-fashioned term," Jameson told author Liz Kahn in her 1996 book on the LPGA. "I cried a lot at her death, for everyone needs someone in her corner, and my mother was a great motivator. Maybe I didn't have the same stimulus after that."

Because tournament play was virtually suspended during World War II, Jameson held jobs that included a stint on the copy desk of *The Dallas Times Herald.* In 1945, she joined the fledgling WPGA and accepted an offer from the Spalding Company to turn professional and perform clinics.

In 1946, the WPGA put on the first U.S. Women's Open in Spokane, in which Jameson was defeated by Patty Berg in the final, 5 and 4, the only time the championship was contested at match play. The next year, at the Starmount Forest Country Club in Greensboro, N.C., Jameson became the first woman to break 300 for 72 holes, her 295 total winning by six strokes. She was runner-up again in 1952.

When the LPGA was started in 1948, Jameson, along with Patty Berg, Louise Suggs and Babe Didrickson Zaharias, made up the Tour's "Big Four." However, Jameson wasn't as inspired by the professional game as she had been as an amateur. Among her 10 victories were the 1949 Texas Open, the 1952 World Championship, the 1954 Western Open. Her best year was 1955, when she won four tournaments. Although she played until 1963, she never won again.

"I loved my career, though I think it was a little time-wasting," said Jameson, who after retiring from competition taught golf and made a living as a painter. "I didn't dream that without match play the whole essence and drama of golf would disappear. I didn't realize how humdrum it is, playing hole after hole and not daring to take chances."

In 1951, Jameson was named one of the 11 charter members of the LPGA Hall of Fame. It was Jameson who conceived the idea of annually honoring the player with the best scoring average on the LPGA Tour and, in 1952, donated the trophy that would become the Vare Trophy in honor of her idol, Glenna Collett Vare.

THE JAMESON RECORD

Major Championship Victories . . . 5

U.S. Amateur: 1939, 1940, 1942

U.S. Women's Open: 1947

Women's Western Open: 1954

Leading Money Winner: 1947, 1953

Willie Anderson

Willie Anderson's place in U.S. Open history belongs on the same pantheon as Bobby Jones, Ben Hogan and Jack Nicklaus. He was the first to win four U.S. Open Championships and the only golfer in history to win three in succession. The sad part of Anderson's biography is that he died at age 30 from what has been described as an overindulgent lifestyle. Since his death in 1910, just two golfers – Hogan (1950, 1951) and Curtis Strange (1988, 1989) – have won two consecutive Opens, and only Hogan has come close to winning four out of five years, as Anderson did in 1901, 1903, 1904 and 1905.

Alex Smith, a Scotsman who finished second to Anderson in two U.S. Opens, believed that, "Most likely, had he lived longer, Willie would have set a record for Open championships that would never be beaten." From 1897 to 1910, Anderson won the Open four times, finished second once, third once, fourth once and fifth three times. He also won the Western Open four times, which at the time was considered a major championship.

Reared on the links of North Berwick, Scotland, Anderson was a sturdy man, with muscular shoulders, brawny forearms and exceptionally large hands. He played with a flat, full-sweeping action that was charactertistic of the Scots and known as the "St. Andrews swing." Despite what many considered to be swing flaws, Anderson was consistently accurate. Gene Sarazen was once practicing bunker shots when another pro casually asked him if Willie Anderson could have gotten out of those bunkers as well as he was doing. "Get out of them?" Sarazen said. "He was never in them!"

Anderson's first U.S. Open victory came at Myopia Hunt Club in 1901. Using a gutta percha ball, he defeated Joe Lloyd in the first playoff in Open history. Five strokes down with five holes to play, Anderson finished 4-4-4-4-4 to defeat Lloyd 85 to 86. It was payback for the 1897 Open, where Lloyd hit a brassie to eight feet on the closing hole and made the putt to defeat the 17-year-old Anderson. It was also a showcase for Anderson to make a stand for social change. The custom was for the professionals to eat their lunch in the clubhouse kitchen, but Anderson would not stand for that. "Nae, nae, we're nae goin' t' eat in the kitchen," he said, swinging his club and taking a divot out of the club's lawn. A compromise was reached: Myopia erected a tent, and the pros ate there.

After finishing fifth in 1902, Anderson went on his historic run. He won at Baltusrol — where he was host professional — in 1903 in a playoff against Deacon Davey Brown. The next year, Anderson set the Open scoring record by shooting 303 to win by five strokes over Gil Nicholls at Glen View Golf Club. In 1905, Anderson completed his hat trick by making up a five-stroke deficit with 36 holes to play at Myopia. His streak ended in 1906 at Onwentsia, where, needing 72 in the final round, he staggered home in 84.

Anderson was modest in nature, never boasting about the level of his play, always letting his game speak for itself. For this, he developed a reputation for being dour. "You couldn't tell whether he was winning or losing by looking at him," said Fred McLeod, the U.S. Open champion of 1908.

Unlike J.H. Taylor and Harold Hilton, he never wrote an instructional book, but he taught effectively and many aspiring amateurs worshipped him. He died in 1910, five years after winning his fourth Open. The official cause of his death was arteriosclerosis, a hardening of the arteries.

"How good was Willie Anderson?" wrote Robert Sommers in the USGA's *Golf Journal*. "Those who played against him and watched the great players of later years said he was as good as anyone who ever played."

THE ANDERSON RECORD

Major Championship Victories 4
U.S. Open: 1901, 1903, 1904, 1905

Other Significant Victories
Western Open: 1902, 1904, 1908, 1909

Fred Corcoran

You won't find his name in any golf record book, but Fred Corcoran was one of golf's pioneers. In the years following World War II, Corcoran helped found the Ladies Professional Golf Association, the World Cup and the Golf Writers Association of America. His idea helped spawn the World Golf Hall of Fame, and he was one of the sport's first agents, managing the careers of Babe Zaharias, Tony Lema and Sam Snead. But perhaps the biggest imprint Corcoran left on the game was that, for a decade, he guided tournament golf in this country into its Golden Age.

Part idea man, part hustler, part mover-and-shaker, part publicist, all-around good guy, Corcoran was as much a fixture in golf during his heyday than any of the players. He had a sharp mind, a great sense of timing and all the connections. If golf writers wanted an anecdote, a quote, or a stat, they went to Corcoran. If tournaments wanted a player, they went to Corcoran. If players wanted representation, they went to Corcoran. For a while, it seemed like he was the center of golf's universe.

Corcoran was nine when he got his first job in golf, caddying at Belmont C.C. near Boston. He advanced to caddy master at age 12, and kept moving up. As a teenager, he served as Belmont's assistant golf secretary, and later as executive secretary for the Massachusetts Golf Association. It was in this role that Corcoran turned tournament scoring into an art form. By using an elaborate, multicolored crayon system, Corcoran was able to keep spectators and the media up to date on the tournament's progress. The United States Golf Association took notice and made Corcoran the official scorer for its events.

From there, Corcoran went to Pinehurst, where he worked as an assistant golf secretary in the office of Donald Ross, the golf course architect. His career took off in 1937, when the PGA of America hired him to replace Bob Harlow as tournament manager of the professional TOUR. The only problem the PGA had with Harlow was that he was wearing too many hats. With Corcoran, who was then only 28, the stipulation was that he would concentrate solely on running and promoting the TOUR. He was paid $5,000 a year, plus $5 a day in expense money.

But Corcoran's timing was always incredible. Shortly after he was hired, a young Virginian named Sam Snead won the Oakland Open and became a hot commodity. Tempted by a series of lucrative exhibitions, Snead was ready to skip the Phoenix Open and collect the guaranteed money. Corcoran went to PGA President George Jacobus, who told Corcoran to sign Snead to a manager's contract and advise him to play Phoenix. For the next 40 years, he handled the career of Snead, and others, including baseball's Ted Williams and Stan Musial.

As golf's P.T. Barnum, Corcoran sold golf to America. He raised the men's annual purses from $150,000 to $750,000 within 10 years, then moved on. In 1948, he put together the struggling Women's Professional Golf Association with Wilson Sporting Goods, and this led to the formation of the LPGA. Three years later, Corcoran and John Jay Hopkins put together the International Golf Association, which led to the an event called the Canada Cup, which later became the World Cup. His inclusion in the World Golf Hall of Fame, needs no further explaining. Fred Corcoran was golf.

THE CORCORAN RECORD

Official Scorer for 34 USGA Championships
Tournament Manager, PGA: 1937-1948
Manager, Ryder Cup Team: 1937, 1939, 1953
Founder, Golf Writers Association of America: 1946
Founder, LPGA: 1948
LPGA Director: 1949-1961
Promotional Director, PGA: 1952-1955
William D. Richardson Award: 1960

Joe Dey

There has been no golf administrator who had a greater influence on the game of golf than Joseph C. Dey, Jr.

His was a 40 year run that brought about sweeping change, and was executed in the most dignified manner. Dey served as Executive Director of the United States Golf Association from 1935-1969, and then as Commissioner of the PGA TOUR from 1969-1974. The following year, he was named captain of the Royal and Ancient Golf Club of St. Andrews, Scotland, the game's highest honorary position. It is unlikely that anyone else will ever again hold these three positions.

"Joe was a man of great integrity, one who was respected by players, officials and everyone in the game," said Michael Bonallack, Secretary of the Royal and Ancient Golf Club of St. Andrews. "I found you could learn a lot from Joe — not just about golf, but about life."

Dey was the first to popularize the Rules of Golf. He set about expanding interest in and knowledge of the Rules of Golf by producing a series of 8-mm films and publications such as *Golf Rules in Pictures*, and the wallet-sized card referred to as *Golf Rules in Brief*. He was known as "Mr. Rules of Golf," but this was just the opening paragraph in his list of accomplishments.

It was Dey, Richard Tufts and Isaac Grainger that brought together the USGA with the R&A, unifying the Rules at a conference in Great Britain in 1951. It was Dey who was entrusted with U.S. Open course set-up decisions. These included the feature of changing reachable par-5s into Herculean par-4s, the implementation of gallery rope at Baltusrol in 1954 and the use of a more sophisticated scoring system. It was also under Dey's administration that five more USGA Championships, including the Women's Open, were added to the schedule, along with the development of its Green Section, the establishment of a velocity regulation to curb ball distance, the move to "Golf House," the building of a USGA Museum and Library, and the foundation of the World Amateur Council.

It was a surprise when he left the USGA at age 61 to head the newly formed Tournament Players Division of the Professional Golfers Association, but Dey felt he had a unique opportunity to create something beneficial to golf. At the time, the TOUR was in turmoil, having just broken from the PGA of America after a prolonged dispute. It was a public relations nightmare for the touring professionals, but Dey brought the TOUR respectability and stability. "Joe was one of the few people that both sides would accept," said Jack Tuthill, the TOUR's former manager and director of tournament operations.

With just $45,000 to work with, Dey steered the ship through the hard times until Deane Beman could take over in 1974. THE PLAYERS Championship was Dey's idea, as was the formation of a secondary tour, now known as the NIKE TOUR, and the mandate that tournament sponsors employ a USGA agronomist to standardize playing conditions.

Born in Norfolk, Va., on Nov. 17, 1907, Dey considered entering the ministry before deciding to make golf administration his career. He always carried two books in the pocket of his blue blazer, the Rules of Golf and the New Testament. He lived by the words of both. "In the world of golf," former USGA President William C. Campbell once said, "Joe Dey was the mightiest oak of all."

THE DEY RECORD

Executive Director, USGA: 1935-1968

Secretary, World Amateur Golf Council: 1958-1969

William D. Richardson Award: 1961

Commissioner, PGA TOUR: 1969-1974

Captain, Royal and Ancient Golf Club of St. Andrews: 1975

Bob Jones Award: 1977

Charles 'Chick' Evans

Charles "Chick" Evans was the first man to win the U.S. Open and the U.S. Amateur in the same year. Using seven hickory-shafted clubs, Evans led the 1916 Open at Minikahda from start to finish, shooting a record score of 286 that would stand for 20 years. Ten weeks later, at Merion, he won the Amateur by beating Bob Gardner, the defending champion, in the final. The only other golfer in history to win these two tournaments in the same year was Bobby Jones, who did it in 1930, the year of his Grand Slam.

Gene Sarazen said that, "in his day, Chick Evans was a finer iron-player than any of the professionals." Henry Cotton called Evans "undoubtedly the greatest amateur golfer of his generation." And Jones, after losing to Evans in match play, said that "Chick is one of the gamest and best competitive golfers the world ever saw."

Evans also endured despite an ongoing battle with his putting stroke. He competed in every Amateur from 1907 through 1962, winning again in 1920, defeating Francis Ouimet in the final. He was medalist in 1909, advanced to the second round in 1955 against a field that included 15-year-old Jack Nicklaus, was a finalist on three other occasions and holds the record for most matches won (57).

His overall record was just phenomenal: eight Western Amateurs, a Western Open, a North and South, a French Amateur, and a runner-up finish in the 1914 Open, where he lost by a stroke to Walter Hagen.

Yet Evans never felt that his achievements were given their just due. According to historians, he resented Ouimet and Jerome Travers because they were the first two amateurs to win the Open, and later in his career, he fell into the shadow cast by Jones. It was unfortunate, because Evans had a 15-year run where he was as good as any golfer in the world, professional or amateur.

Evans had some peculiar philosophies. "I made a rule never to swing a golf club except to hit a golf ball," he said, "for I had learned that one could swing beautifully when the ball wasn't there, and poorly when it was." He also had his own theory on practice. "Most people seem to consider playing as practice and that is one of the reasons that they never emerge from the heap," he said. "There is a vast difference between practicing golf shots and playing the game of golf."

Evans's legacy involves more than tournament golf. His name is synonomous with the Western Golf Association, and the institution of the Evans Scholars Foundation. This idea was born after Evans won the Open and the Amateur in 1916. Rather than turn professional, Evans decided to take the $5,000 offered to him for making golf instructional phonograph records and establish a golf scholarship fund for caddies. Through funds generated by the Motorola Western Open and private donations, over 840 scholarships were awarded to caddies in 1997-1998 who met the high academic requirements and have a proven need for financial aid. Since 1930, the Evans Scholars Fund had awarded 8,240 scholarships.

Evans was himself a caddy at Edgewater Golf Club, while growing up on Chicago's North Side, and it was that background which helped mold him into one of the game's most popular players. Eventually, his bitterness toward Ouimet, Travers and Jones subsided, and he developed into the type of golfer who joked with people in the gallery, remembered names and faces, and knew how to smile, win or lose.

THE EVANS RECORD

Major Championship Victories. 3
  U.S. Amateur: 1916, 1920
  U.S. Open: 1916
  (Played in 49 U.S. Amateur
    Championships, winning 57 matches.)
Other Significant Victories
  Western Amateur: 8 times
  North and South Amateur: 1911
  French Amateur: 1911
Walker Cup Teams 3
  (3-2-0) 1922, 1924, 1928
Bob Jones Award: 1960

Young Tom Morris

Young Tom Morris followed in his father's footsteps, winning four British Open Championships, before his tragic death at the age of 24. With broad shoulders, and hands that were both powerful and deft, he dominated the game in the short time he played it. "He was simply too good for the available competition," wrote Ross Goodner in *Golf's Greatest*. That included his father, Old Tom, whom he succeeded as Open champion in 1868. The following year, Old Tom finished runner-up to his son. It is the only time in major championship history that a son and his father finished first and second.

Young Tom was a prodigy. At 13, he won an exhibition match in Perth for a first prize of £15. At 16, Morris won the Open Professional Tournament at Carnoustie against the best golfers in Scotland. At 17, he became the tournament's youngest winner and began his domination of the Open, winning three consecutive titles to take permanent possession of the Championship Belt in 1870. That was the year he shot 149 over Prestwick's 12-hole course, a score that was 12 strokes better than the competition and unequalled by the Great Triumverate of James Braid, J.H. Taylor and Harry Vardon while the gutta percha ball was in use. His opening round of 47 that year, one-under 4s, included an eagle 3 at the 578-yard first, and has been described as the first great round of golf. H.S.C. Everard speculated, "It is probable that Tommy attained a rare pitch of excellence at as early an age as any golfer on record."

The Open wasn't played in 1871, but Morris made it four in a row in 1872, which is a record. That victory also gained Young Tom Morris the distinction of being the first golfer to win the silver claret jug, the permanent trophy for the Open Championship.

Tall, strong and incredible handsome, Young Tom was to golf in his era what Arnold Palmer became in the late 1950s. It was said he sometimes inadvertently snapped a shaft in two merely by waggling the clubhead, but he also displayed an uncanny finesse around the greens. "Young Tom Morris brought to the game a flamboyance that it had never known," wrote Charles Price in *The World of Golf*.

Like his father, Tom Morris, Jr., was idolized not only for the way he played, but the way he competed. In *St. Andrews: Home of Golf*, Young Tom was described as "endearingly modest." Robert Clark, author of *Golf: A Royal and Ancient Game*, wrote about Morris's "amiable temperament…obliging disposition…gentlemanly appearance…manly bearing," and "undaunted determination." Today, he would be described as having the total package. "Golfers may come and golfers may go, but it is very much open to doubt whether any golfers will be quite the idol of the day as Young Tom was during his brilliant career," wrote Harold Hutchinson in *The Book of Golf and Golfers*.

His life came to an end in 1875. Playing an exhibition match with his father in North Berwick against Willie and Mungo Park, Morris received a telegram that his wife of a year and son had both died during childbirth. It was a mournful party that made the voyage across the Firth of Forth to St. Andrews, and Morris never recovered from the shock of his loss. He died three months later, on Christmas Eve, of what has been described as a broken heart. His memory is perpetuated by a plaque in St. Andrews Cathedral which bears the inscription, "Deeply regretted by numerous friends and all golfers, he thrice in succession won the championship belt and held it without rivalry and yet without envy, his many amiable golfing qualities being no less acknowledged than his golfing achievements."

THE YOUNG TOM MORRIS RECORD

Major Championship Victories . . . 4

British Open: 1868, 1869, 1870, 1872

In his victory in 1868, he was the first to record a hole-in-one in a major championship.

J.H. Taylor

It was the legendary Scotsman, Andrew Kirkaldy, who first saw the greatness in John Henry Taylor. After losing a challenge match to Taylor in 1891, Kirkaldy went back to St. Andrews and predicted that the young Englishman who just defeated him would win many Open Championships. "You'll see more of Taylor," he said. "And then you'll know why he beat me, and why he will beat all the best of the day."

Kirkaldy proved to be right, of course. Three years after defeating Kirkaldy, he became the first Englishman to win the Open. Taylor went on to win five British Opens, joining Harry Vardon and James Braid to form the Great Triumvirate.

Taylor's accuracy was legendary. At Sandwich, where he won his first Open by five strokes in 1894, he would have the directional posts removed from the blind holes out of fear that his drives would hit them and carom into bunkers. The following year, he won by four strokes over Sandy Herd at St. Andrews, with Kirkaldy six shots farther back in third place.

"The mon's a machine," Kirkaldy said. "He can dae naething wrang."

Vardon and amateur Harold Hilton came along to dominate the Open from 1896-99, but Taylor returned to form in 1900 at St. Andrews. Pulling away from the field after every round, he ended up winning by eight strokes over Vardon, with Braid 13 back in third place. Later in the year, he finished second to Vardon in the U.S. Open at Chicago Golf Club.

Taylor would win the British Open twice more, both times in convincing manner, in 1909 over Braid at Deal and in 1913 over Ted Ray at Hoylake. The latter tied Taylor with Braid and Vardon with five Open victories and was considered his most satisfying win since it came in horrendous conditions. In heavy wind and rain, Taylor pulled his cap down over his eyes, stuck out his chin, and anchored his large boots to the ground to maximize control over his compact swing. Nineteen years after his first Open victory, Taylor shot 304 to win by eight strokes over Ray, the defending champion.

Taylor took the game ultra seriously, and once wrote: "To try to play golf really well is far from being a joke, and lightheartedness of endeavor is a sure sign of eventual failure." Bernard Darwin, who was a close friend, recalled that nobody, not even Bobby Jones, suffered more over championships than Taylor did. "Like Bobby," said Darwin, "(Taylor) had great control and might appear outwardly cool, but the flames leaped up from within."

Taylor was competitive for many years, finishing fourth at the age of 53 in the 1924 British Open at Hoylake. Most of his later life was dedicated to writing books, making clubs, designing courses and forming the British PGA, the Artisan Golfers Association and the Public Golf Courses Association. As a young boy, he left school early to caddy and work as a gardener's assistant, a mason's laborer and a greenkeeper. But he educated himself by reading Dickens and Boswell, and was able to author *Golf, My Life's Work*, without a ghostwriter. He took great pride in having grown up an Englishman, on the links of Westward Ho! rather than the links of St. Andrews or East Lothian in Scotland.

Taylor's final years were spent in his native village of Northam overlooking Westward Ho!, enjoying the view he called "the finest in Christendom." His death in 1963 just short of his 92nd birthday marked the passing of the last of the great golfers from the 19th century.

THE TAYLOR RECORD

Major Championship Victories . . . 5
  British Open: 1894, 1895, 1900, 1909, 1913

Other Significant Victories
  British Match Play: 1908
  French Open: 1908, 1909
  German Open: 1912

Ryder Cup (Non-Playing Captain): 1933

Glenna Collett Vare

Glenna Collett Vare was known as the female Bobby Jones. She was the greatest female golfer of her day, but equally important as the number of times she won, was the way she won. As Jones once wrote, "Aside from her skill with her clubs, Miss Collett typified all that the word 'sportsmanship' stands for." Renowned as the "Queen of American Golf," Vare won a record six U.S. Women's Amateur Championships, two Canadian Women's Opens, and a French Women's Open in an era when there was no Ladies Professional Golf Association Tour. She did it with style and dignity, raising the awareness of women's golf in a country that didn't know the sport existed. "Glenna was the first woman," said former USGA President Richard Tufts, "to attack the hole rather than just play to the green."

In 1924, Collett won 59 out of 60 matches, losing only on the 19th hole of the semifinal of the Women's Amateur when Mary K. Browne's ball caromed off hers and into the cup. Joyce Wethered of Great Britain was Collett Vare's only equal, and even she admitted that when Glenna was on her game, nobody could touch her. "If she is finding her true form, then there is little hope, except by miracle, of surviving," Wethered wrote in her book *Golfing Memories and Methods*. It was Wethered, however, who handed Collett her most disappointing loss, coming back from five down after 11 holes to win the 1929 Ladies' British Open Amateur Championship. "Her charm to my mind as a golfer and a companion lies in a freedom of spirit which does not make her feel that success is everything in the world," said Wethered.

What made Collett Vare such a dominant player was the prodigious length she hit the ball. One of her drives was measured at 307 yards, and she used this strength to overpower the competition. She won and qualified with scores that were 10 strokes lower than women had been scoring previous to World War I. Enid Wilson, who played against Collett Vare in the Curtis Cup, marveled how Glenna could hit the ball harder than any woman in America had done before. "Her vigorous game set up an entirely fresh standard for her countrywomen, and the young up-and-coming golfers in the 1930s were inspired by her example," said Wilson.

Born in New Haven, Conn., on June 20, 1903, and raised in Providence, R.I., Collett didn't start playing golf until she was 14. Taught by former British Open champion Alex Smith at the Metacomet Club, she won the Amateur for the first time in at age 19. Her final U.S. Women's Amateur victory came as Mrs. Edwin H. Vare, Jr., when she was a 32-year-old mother of two against 17-year-old Patty Berg. Although the LPGA gives its Vare Trophy to the player with the low stroke average on its Tour, most of Vare's victories came in match play. She won the North and South six times, the Eastern Amateur seven times and was 4-2-1 as a player and player-captain in the Curtis Cup, an event she helped originate.

"To make oneself a successful match-player, there are certain qualities to be sought after, certain ideas must be kept in mind, and certain phases of one's attitude towards the game that come in for special notice," Collett Vare once said. "The three I have taken are these: love of combat, serenity of mind and fearlessness."

THE VARE RECORD

Major Championship Victories . . . 6
  U.S. Women's Amateur: 1922, 1925, 1928, 1929, 1930, 1935

Other Significant Victories
  Canadian Amateur: 1923, 1924
  French Amateur: 1925

Eastern Women's Championship: 7 times

North and South Amateur: 6 times

Curtis Cup Teams 5
  (4-2-1) 1932, 1934, 1936, 1938, 1948
  Captain 1934, 1936

Joyce Wethered

She combined feminine grace with the type of precision no golfer of her era was able to achieve. She amazed three time British Open winner Henry Cotton with her ball-striking, and Glenna Collett Vare with her tenacity. Joyce Wethered, who later went by the more proper married name of Lady Heathcoat-Armory, was revered as the queen of British amateur golf. Bob Jones considered her to be the best golfer, man or woman, he had seen.

Wethered won the Ladies' British Open Amateur Championship four times, the English champion five times in a row, and was a leading force in the founding of the Curtis Cup.

Jones had the opportunity to play with Wethered from the back tees before the British Amateur at St. Andrews in 1930. With a breeze blowing off the sea, Wethered did not miss a shot, half heartedly three-putted the 17th from 12 feet after the match was over, and went around the Old Course in 75. It was as clean a round of golf as Jones had ever seen.

"I have not played golf with anyone, man or woman, amateur or professional, who made me feel so utterly outclassed," said Jones. "It was not so much the score she made as the way she made it. It was impossible to expect that Miss Wethered would ever miss a shot — and she never did."

Cotton played in an exhibition with Wethered after she married Sir John Heathcoat-Armory in 1937. She hit the ball 240 yards off the tee, and could play low-flying shots with the mashie that exhibited brilliant touch. Some felt that at her best, Wethered could play No. 4 or No. 5 on the British Walker Cup team, and Cotton seemed to agree. "In my time, no golfer has stood out so far ahead or his or contemporaries as Lady Heathcoat-Armory," said Cotton. "I do not think a golf ball has ever been hit, except perhaps by Harry Vardon, with such a straight flight by any other person."

Wethered established her reputation in this country by twice thwarting the efforts of *Collett* in the British Ladies' Amateur. Their first match occurred at Troon in 1925, just after Collett had won her second U.S. Women's Amateur and the French Open Championship. "The match anticipated between her and myself was worked up to such a pitch beforehand that, when the day came, one of two things was almost bound to happen. Either we should rise to the occasion or one of us would fall under the strain of it."

It was Wethered who rose — making four birdies in 15 holes — and Collett who fell, by a score of 4 and 3. Wethered went on to defeat Cecil Leitch in the final for her third British Ladies' Amateur title. Four years later, Wethered and Collett met again in the final at St. Andrews. Wethered was coming out of a three-year retirement, but Collett was coming off her fourth of five U.S. Women's Amateur titles. With an outward nine of 34, Collett went 5 up. At the 12th, she had a 3-footer to go 6 up and missed. Slowly the holes began to come back, and at the lunch break, Collett was only 2 up. Bernard Darwin wrote that the general impression of the British people was, "It's all right now. You'll see. Joyce will win comfortably."

The 3-and-1 defeat of Collett indicates that Wethered did, indeed, win comfortably. They met again in the inaugural Curtis Cup, with the police clearing the road home for the two heroines. Wethered returned home to England, where the only competition she played was the Worplesdon mixed foursomes, an event she won eight times with seven different partners.

THE WETHERED RECORD

Major Championship Victories 4
British Women's Amateur: 1922, 1924, 1925, 1929

Other Significant Victories
English Ladies' Championship: 1920, 1921, 1922, 1923, 1924

Curtis Cup Teams 1
(1-1-0) 1932
Captain 1932

Tommy Armour

Tommy Armour was the second of only eight golfers in history to win the U.S. Open, the British Open and the PGA Championship. The Silver Scot followed Walter Hagen and Jim Barnes, and preceeded Gene Sarazen, Ben Hogan, Jack Nicklaus, Gary Player, and Lee Trevino, finishing his career just a Masters victory short of achieving the career Grand Slam. While not achieving the ultimate measure of golfing greatness, Armour did, however, win the Western Open, an event then regarded as a major championship, as well as three Canadian Opens and 14 other events in the United States. The Scotsman was considered a closer who played his best golf on the toughest golf courses. Known as an exceptional striker of the ball, and one of the finest wood club players of all time, Armour played the game with a conservative philosophy: "It is not solely the capacity to make great shots that makes champions, but the essential quality of making very few bad shots."

In 1927, Armour won the first U.S. Open played at Oakmont by finishing with five pars and a birdie, then defeating Harry Cooper in an 18-hole playoff. His next major championship victory came in the 1930 PGA at Fresh Meadows on Long Island. Armour lost five of the first six holes against Johnny Farrell in the quarterfinal, but came back to win, 2 and 1. His opponent in the final was Sarazen, who was playing on his home course. All square going to the 36th hole, Armour won with a par. The following year, he won the first British Open played at Carnoustie, shooting 71 in the final round. It was considered to be Armour's finest moment, since the victory was recorded close to his birthplace in Edinburgh.

Bernard Darwin was most impressed with Armour's ability to strike a golf ball. "I do not believe that (J.H.) Taylor or (Harry) Vardon at their best ever gave themselves so many possible putts for three with their iron shots as he does," Darwin once wrote. "His style is the perfection of rhythm and beauty."

In *The Story of American Golf*, Herbert Warren Wind described Armour's uncanny ability to finish out a tournament: "Whenever the Silver Scot played himself into a contending position, he always seemed to have that extra something that was the difference between barely losing and barely winning. He was singularly unaffected by the pressure of the last stretch. His hands were hot but his head was cool."

After he retired from competitive golf, Armour became one of the most successful instructors and golf club designers in the world. Based at Winged Foot in the summer, and the Boca Raton Hotel in the winter, Armour taught both duffers and the world's best golfers, using the same philosophies and techniques that were part of his best-selling book, *How to Play Your Best Golf All the Time*. Julius Boros called him a genius at teaching you how to play your best golf. Lawson Little claimed that Armour was responsible for whatever success he had in golf.

The great golf writer, Charles Price, described Armour as having "a dash of indifference, a touch of class, (and) a bit of majesty." In *Golf's Greatest*, Ross Goodner wrote that "Nothing was ever small about Tommy Armour's reputation. At one time or another, he was known as the greatest iron player, the greatest raconteur, the greatest drinker and the greatest and most expensive teacher in golf." Some called him dour and temperamental, yet Bobby Cruickshank claimed to know Armour for 60 years, and said, "He was the kindest, best-hearted fellow you ever saw."

Certainly, Tommy Armour was a complex man, and misunderstood, but he seemed to like it that way.

THE ARMOUR RECORD

Major Championship Victories . . . 3
  U.S. Open: 1927
  British Open: 1931
  PGA: 1930
Other Significant Victories
  Canadian Open: 1927, 1930, 1934
  Western Open: 1929
PGA TOUR Victories 24

James Braid

He swung with a divine fury, and putted like a demon. Without him, there would not have been a Great Triumverate. But James Braid's contributions to golf are not just based on his five British Open victories, and his place in history next to Harry Vardon and J.H. Taylor. He was a man of great character, who was a friend of princes, peers and commoners. He also left behind one of the world's great golf courses and was a pioneer in elevating the status of professional golfers by helping to form the British PGA.

As a golfer, Braid was considered to be a late bloomer. He did not win his first British Open Championship, in 1901, until Vardon and Taylor had already won three each. But once Braid won his first, there was no stopping him: He captured the Open again in 1905, 1906, 1908 and 1910, thus becoming the first man to raise the old claret jug five times.

The difference between Braid's winning and just finishing among the contenders at the Open was an aluminum-headed putter made by Mills of Sunderland that came into his possession after the 1900 Open at St. Andrews. He had finished sixth in 1896, second in 1897, fifth in 1899 and third in 1900. Once the putts began to fall, Braid began to rise ahead of Vardon and Taylor. In fact, it was Taylor who said, "I have yet to meet the player who could hole the 10-yard putts with greater regularity" than Braid.

And when Braid won, he won by large margins. At Muirfield in 1901, he began with a drive out of bounds at the first hole, but from there on he played superb golf to defeat Vardon by three strokes and Taylor by four. At St. Andrews in 1905, he sailed to a five-stroke victory over Taylor. At Muirfield in 1906, he triumphed by four strokes over Taylor. His greatest performance came at Prestwick in 1908, when he shot the Open record of 291 to win by eight strokes over Tom Ball. That record stood until Bob Jones broke it by six strokes at St. Andrews in 1927. Braid finished runner-up to Taylor in 1909, but came back the next year at St. Andrews to win his fourth Open in six years, this time by four strokes over Alexander Herd.

In 1904, he was also the first player in an Open to break 70, shooting 69 in the third round at Royal St. George's.

Born in Fife, Scotland, in 1870, Braid grew up in humble circumstances. His father worked behind a plow in the farming town about 15 miles south of St. Andrews called Earlsferry, and did not play golf or promote his son's interest in the sport. Braid left school at 13 to become an apprentice joiner, sneaking in rounds of golf on his travels. Three years later he was a scratch player, and at 23 he moved to London and became a clubmaker, working at the Army and Navy Stores for eight pence an hour. His golf came after work and on Sunday. Eight years later, he began his remarkable string of British Open victories.

In his later years, Braid remained competitive. After World War I, he was still good enough to play in the first Britain vs. America matches, and in 1927, at the age of 57, fought his way into the final of the British Match Play Championship. At that point in his life, Braid was playing most of his golf at Walton Heath, where he served as head professional for 45 years. He also enjoyed a successful career as a golf course architect, designing such lasting treasures as Carnoustie and the King's and Queen's courses at Gleneagles. James Braid died in London in 1950.

THE BRAID RECORD

Major Tournament Victories 5
British Open: 1901, 1905, 1906,
1908, 1910

Other Significant Victories
British Professional Match Play:
1903, 1905, 1907, 1911
French Open: 1910

Old Tom Morris

Old Tom Morris didn't invent the game of golf, but he is recognized as the sport's founding father. He played in the first 36 British Opens, winning four times, and sired a son, Tom Morris, Jr., who won the world's oldest golf championship four times on his own. But as much as his successes in tournament golf and as a parent are significant, Tom Morris, Sr., left behind the legacy of being a champion among men.

The authors of the day came to respect him for the way he handled victory as well as defeat; and there was no greater loss than when Tom Morris, Jr., mourning the death of his wife and child, died at the age of 24. Horace Hutchinson wrote about Morris's "unruffled serenity of temper." John L. Low described the way Morris was "always cheerful during a life which met with almost continual disappointments and sorrows." Yet, according to Hutchinson and Low, what separated Old Tom was his humbleness, and the way he addressed himself to men of all classes.

In *The Book of Golf and Golfers*, Hutchinson described him as "One of the most remarkable men — best of men and best of golfers — that ever missed a short putt." Hutchinson concluded that Morris "has been written of as often as a Prime Minister, he has been photographed as often as a professional beauty, and yet he remains, through all the advertisement, exactly the same, simple and kindly."

Born in St. Andrews, Scotland, on June 16, 1820, Morris spent 12 years as a golf-ball maker under Allan Robertson before moving to Prestwick, where he became custodian of the newly formed club that, in 1860, gave birth to the British Open. He finished second to Willie Park in the first Open Championship, won the next two, finished

second to Park again in 1863, then won again in 1864 and 1867. He had a slow, smooth swing and was fiercely competitive; his only flaw was a difficulty with short putts. In 1862, he didn't miss many, winning the Open by 13 strokes, a record that still stands.

Morris moved back to St. Andrews in 1865 to become greenkeeper for the Royal and Ancient Golf Club. It was a position he held until his retirement in 1904. Today, his portrait hangs in the R&A Clubhouse and the 18th green of the Old Course is named in his memory. He is revered today not only as a golfer, but as a course designer — he had a hand in Prestwick, Royal Dornoch, Muirfield and Carnoustie, among other great Scottish courses — and statesman. It was the way Old Tom Morris carried himself that defined the sport as a gentleman's game.

"As St. Andrews became increasingly a mecca of golfers, so too did the sturdy patriarchal figure and bearing of Old Tom come to symbolize all that was finest in the Scottish character and in the ancient Scottish game," wrote James K. Robertson in *St. Andrews, Home of Golf.* "His kindly, yet capable and gentle nature, enshrined him a good many years before his death as the authentic Grand Old Man of Golf. To generations of people all over the world his name and his picture epitomized the game."

When Morris died, in 1908 at the age of 87, the funeral procession extended the entire length of South Street in St. Andrews, from the port to the cathedral. It was described by Andrew Kirkaldy as "a cloud of people," and as Kirkaldy noted, "there were many wet eyes among us, for Old Tom was beloved by everybody."

THE MORRIS SR. RECORD

Major Championship Victories 4

British Open: 1861, 1862, 1864, 1867

Greenskeeper at St. Andrews:
1865-1904

Golf course architecture, he designed or remodeled 75 courses.

Jerome D. Travers

Some of the words used to describe Jerry Travers have not been kind — cold, somber, ruthless — yet these were the qualities that made him the most feared golfer of his time. In a nine-year stretch from 1906-1915, Travers won four U.S. Amateurs, five Metropolitan Amateurs and a U.S. Open. Only Bob Jones won more major amateur titles, and Travers was one of only five amateurs to win the Open. His battles with Walter Travis, in the words of Herbert Warren Wind, "formed the crucible in which a talented young golfer was made into the greatest match player of his decade."

Yet, in assessing his career, the words unfulfilled and disappointing have been used, too. The truth is, Jerry Travers never became a true hero of American golf, and his accomplishments are the least remembered among history's greats. Why? For the same reasons that Travers was so successful, and also because his run of greatness concluded so abruptly. Although he lived to 61, Travers's championship career came to an end at age 28. In the midst of his heyday, he twice didn't bother to enter the Amateur. And he never entered the Open again after winning in 1915.

Bizarre? Peculiar? Indeed. Jerry Travers had a reputation for being undisciplined off the golf course, and lacking a steadying influence in his life. He also seemed to thrive on being hard to read. "He was anything but an outgoing person," the great amateur Jess Sweetser recalls. "He was totally lacking in what today is called charisma."

Among his peers, however, Travers earned ultimate, almost intimidating, respect. Chick Evans called him "the coldest, hardest golfer I ever knew." Francis Ouimet described him as "the best match player in the country." Alex Smith, the National Open champion who taught Travers, called his student, "the greatest competitor I have ever known."

At only 5-foot-7, and 140 pounds, Travers had to be tough to survive.

One on one, he was so absorbed in his work and the shot at hand that it was impossible to read his emotions. "I could always tell whether a golfer was winning or losing by looking at him," said Smith. "But I never knew how Travers stood."

Neither, sometimes, did Travers. Ouimet recalled the time he beat Travers in the 1914 Amateur, 6 and 5, in the third round: "I waited for Jerry to do the customary handshaking act, but to my surprise he walked to his caddy, selected a driver, and hastened to the next tee. The referee then hustled over to Travers and asked him if he intended to play the bye holes. 'Why?' asked Travers. 'Is the match over?' I was somewhat embarrassed as Jerry apologized for his error, and his congratulations were as warm as they could possibly be."

What also made Travers so great was his ability to putt the ball. Harold Hilton, who defeated Travers on his way to the Amateur title at Apawamis in 1911, called him, "The greatest putter I ever saw." Travers believed that putting was more a combination of the mental and physical than any stroke in the game, and he worked for hours perfecting his method.

What, then, went wrong? It is theorized that a combination of burnout and lifestyle led to the disappearance of Jerry Travers, and although he returned for exhibitions, and later as a teaching professional, he was clearly not the Jerry Travers who relentlessly once dominated the world of amateur golf.

THE TRAVERS RECORD

Major Championship Victories . . . 6
U.S. Amateur: 1907, 1908, 1912, 1913, 1920
U.S. Open: 1915

Other Significant Victories
New Jersey Amateur: 3 times
Metropolitan (New York) Amateur: 5 times

Mickey Wright

Ben Hogan described her swing as the best he ever saw. So did Byron Nelson. For 14 years, she dominated women's golf, winning 82 tournaments, and carrying the Ladies Professional Golf Association Tour on her shoulders. Mickey Wright was not burdened by potential — potential, in her words, was but a hope to be fulfilled. What made her retire, at age 34, was the burden of being Mickey Wright.

"The pressure was so great," remembers Kathy Whitworth. "Sponsors threatened to cancel their tournaments if she didn't play. And, knowing that if they canceled, the rest of us wouldn't be able to play, Mickey would always play."

The buzzword today is burnout. Wright played 33 tournaments in 1962, another 30 in 1963, and 27 in 1964. She won 10, 13 and 11 tournaments those years, and, as the LPGA's president, it was Wright's duty to promote the Tour by doing every conceivable interview and attending every press conference that was scheduled. That just wasn't her. "I'm not real good as far as wanting to be in front of people, glorying in it and loving it," Wright has said. "I think you have to love that to make that kind of pressure tolerable. It finally got to where it wasn't tolerable to me."

It had also reached the point where there wasn't much left to accomplish. Wright won the U.S. Women's Open and the LPGA Championship four times each. She won the Vare Trophy five times, was the leading money winner four times, twice had winning streaks of four-straight tournaments and held LPGA records for lowest round (62), lowest nine-hole score (30) and most birdies in a round (nine). At the peak of her career, Herbert Warren Wind described her as "a tall, good-looking girl who struck the ball with the same decisive hand action that the best men players use, she fused her hitting action smoothly with the rest of her swing, which was like Hogan's in that all the unfunctional moves had been pared away, and like Jones's in that its cohesive timing disguised the effort that went into it."

Citing an adverse reaction to sunlight, an aversion to flying and foot problems, Wright cut back her schedule dramatically after the 1969 season to lead a quieter, simpler life, in Port St. Lucie, Fla. Although she came back in 1973 to win the Dinah Shore, Wright knew that she had fulfilled her potential, and elected to bow out on her terms. "I maintain that she could have won 100 tournaments if she hadn't quit early," says Whitworth, who won 88.

Born on Feb. 14, 1935, in San Diego, Wright began to hit balls with her father at age 4. At the age of 11 she received her first lesson at La Jolla CC, and within a year had broken 100. Three years later, she posted a round of 70 in a local tournament, and, in 1952, Mickey Wright won the USGA Girls' Junior Championship for her first national title.

For a year, Wright studied psychology at Stanford, but she left school after her freshman year to play a fulltime schedule. In the summer of 1954, she lost in the final of the U.S. Women's Amateur, finished fourth in the Women's Open to Babe Zaharias, and won the World Amateur staged by golf promoter George S. May. Those three tournaments convinced Wright to leave school and turn professional.

"Golf has brought me more rewards, financially and personally, than I ever could have earned had I become the psychology teacher I set out to be," Wright said later in life. "I feel as if I've earned my own version of a master's degree in psychology in study and experience, trial and error, on golf courses throughout the United States. For psychology . . . is as integral a part of good golf as an efficient swing."

THE WRIGHT RECORD

Major Championship Victories   13
U.S. Open: 1958, 1959, 1961, 1964
LPGA: 1958, 1960, 1961, 1963
Titleholders: 1961, 1962
Western Open: 1962, 1963, 1966

Other Significant Victories
U.S. Girl's Junior: 1952
World Amateur: 1954

LPGA Tour Victories 84
Vare Trophy: 1960, 1961, 1962, 1963, 1964
Leading Money Winner: 1961, 1962, 1963, 1964
Associated Press Women Athlete of the Year: 1962, 1963

Bobby Locke

Under the category of great putters in golf history, Arthur D'Arcy (Bobby) Locke is certainly at the top of the list — and there are those in a contingent, led by Gary Player, who would argue that the South African was the best of all time. Locke won four British Opens in a span of eight years, and dominated when he did play the PGA TOUR, earning him the distinction as the first great, non-British, non-American golfer. He did it though, with more than just the flat blade.

Locke was described as having a bizarre personality and an unorthodox style. After World War II, he dressed almost exclusively in grey flannel knickers, white buckskin shoes, linen dress shirts with neckties and white Hogan caps. He played the ukulele and had a reputation for being one of the game's great partiers. On the golf course, he moved at a maddeningly slow pace. Large gaps would open in front of him, his playing partners would grow red-necked in anger, officials would threaten penalties, but Locke was unyielding. He never lost his temper or expressed annoyance, and was described as cool, shrewd and imperturbable. The American pros nicknamed him "Muffin Face" because of his changeless expression.

Visually, Locke's golf swing was no work of art. He learned by reading Bobby Jones's instruction books and adapting a wristy inside-out move that consistently produced a hard right-to-left draw. What was so amazing about Locke's shot pattern was its consistency. He rarely missed a green, and when he did, he had the short game and the disposition to save par. This was an adaptation Jones's philosophy that the real secret of success in golf was turning three shots into two.

Using an old rusty-headed putter with a hickory shaft, Locke would even hook his putts. He'd address the ball at the toe and stroke out at it, imparting topspin which resulted in true, end-over-end rotation. He believed in dying the ball in the hole, using the front and the two sides of the cup. "Very early in my career I realized that putting was half the game of golf," Locke said. "No matter how well I might play the long shots, if I couldn't putt, I would never win."

In this country, Locke was nearly unbeatable. In one 32-month span, he played in 59 tournaments, winning 11, finishing second 10 times, third eight times and fourth five times. This led to bad blood among the Americans he was beating, and in 1949, after winning his first British Open, Locke remained in Great Britain to play a series of exhibitions and autumn events. This led to the PGA of America barring Locke because he had committed to play in selected tournaments on the United States TOUR.

Although the ban was lifted, Locke never again felt welcome, and played most of his golf in Europe. He won the Open again in 1950, 1952, and in 1957, to break Peter Thomson's streak of three Open Championships in a row. Two years later, he was involved in a bad roadside accident in South Africa, and it undoubtedly meant he would never be the same golfer again. Bobby Locke died in 1987 at the age of 69 in Johannesburg, South Africa.

THE LOCKE RECORD

Major Championship Victories . . . 4
  British Open: 1949, 1950, 1952, 1957
PGA TOUR Victories 11
European Tour Victories 23
South African Tour Victories . . . 38
Other Significant Victories
  South African Amateur: 1935, 1937
  South African Open: 1935, 1937, 1938, 1939, 1940, 1946, 1950, 1951, 1955
  Irish Open: 1938
  New Zealand Open: 1938
  Dunlop Masters: 1950, 1954
  Egyptian Open: 1954
  Swiss Open: 1954

John Ball

John Ball dominated amateur golf in Great Britain the way Bob Jones did in the United States. He won eight British Amateur championships, a British Open and the hearts and respect of his country. In the words of British golf historian Donald Steel, "No golfer ever came to be more of a legend in his own lifetime." He was the first amateur golfer in England to be named by the Royal Empire as an Immortal.

In 1878, at the age of 14, Ball finished fifth in the British Open held at Prestwick. His run of Amateur titles began in 1888 and stretched until 1912, when he was 51 years old. His best year was 1890, when he won both the British Amateur and Open Championships. Jones, who won the Grand Slam in 1930, is the only other golfer in history to win those two tournaments in the same year.

Although he gripped the club tightly in the palms of both hands, Ball's swing was the most graceful and stylish of his era. Bernard Darwin wrote that, "I have derived greater aesthetic and emotional pleasure from watching John Ball than from any other spectacle in the game."

Ball learned the game competing against Harold Hilton on the links at Hoylake. In 1876, at the age of 15, he competed in his first British Open and finished sixth at St. Andrews. Nine years later, he competed in his first British Amateur, but it wasn't until 1887 that Ball reached the final and lost to Hutchinson. He won his first Amateur title the next year, defeating J.E. Findlay at Prestwick, 5 and 4.

In 1892, Ball defeated Hilton in the final of the British Amateur at Sandwich, but finished runner-up to Hilton in the Open Champinship at Muirfield. He would not get as close again in the Open, but continued to play competitive golf at a high standard into his later years. At age 60 he reached the sixth round of the British Amateur. In 1927, at the age of 66, Ball attempted to win his 100th British Amateur match, but was defeated in the second round and came up one victory shy of the milestone. It wasn't long afterward that Ball retired to a farm in North Wales, where he died in 1940.

Ball was famous for refusing to carry a niblick, which had the loft of a modern day 8- or 9-iron. He scorned the use of that club, describing it as "another bloody spade," and admonished the Rules of Golf Committee of the Royal and Ancient for permitting such horrid-looking contraptions to be allowed in competition. In a bunker, Ball would simply lay open the blade of a mid-iron and float the ball toward the hole with a smooth swing.

It was this stubbornness, and dogged determination, that made Ball such a lion in match play. Darwin once noted that Ball had "a strong vein of hostility and if he wanted a particular player's blood, he would fight his way through a tournament with the sole object of getting at him." Darwin added, "That was not a personal hostility, but rather a desire to measure himself against a foe really worth of him."

Words from Ball are hard to find. He was a shy man who went about his business without wasted motion. In his book, *Sixty Years Of Golf*, Robert Harris wrote that "John's soft, whispering voice, his stoicism, his pawky jibs at easy rules and innovations, his relentless criticism of moderns with their fuss, and his total outlook on the game, were the very essence of golf."

THE BALL RECORD

Major Championship Victories . . . 9
British Amateur: 1888, 1890, 1892,
1894, 1899, 1907, 1910, 1912

British Open: 1890

Herb Graffis

Herb Graffis didn't miss much when he sat down to his typewriter. He was part of a generation of great golf writers that included Grantland Rice, Bernard Darwin, Ring Lardner, Henry Longhurst, Herbert Warren Wind and Charles Price, yet his greatest contributions to the game came not from what he wrote, but through the conception of his ideas.

Along with his brother Joe, Graffis founded the *Chicago Golfer* in 1923, *Golfdom* in 1927 and then a national monthly, *Golfing*, in 1933. They founded the National Golf Foundation, the Golf Course Superintendents Association and the Club Managers Association, and published the first U.S. Open program in 1928 at Olympic Fields.

It was Graffis who believed that golf was a business as well as a game. *Golfdom*, for example, was a magazine with a controlled circulation that was sent to the president, green chairman, professional, greenkeeper and course manager at each club. *Golfing* was created, in Graffis' words, "because the manufacturers couldn't afford to spend much on ad space in the (*Saturday Evening*) *Post* or *Colliers*, but they wanted to do something that would get in the hands of a select list of golfers." *Golfing* was published five times a year and sent out free. The Graffis philosophy was that "the most important guy was the one reading it, not the guy who was being written about."

In 1936, the Graffis brothers nearly went bankrupt forming the National Golf Foundation as a means of helping promote the growth of the game. It was the NGF's mission to research and publish authoritative information on the game which could be used by investors developing the game of golf.

Graffis also collaborated with Tommy Armour on three best-selling instruction books, *How to Play Your Best Golf All The Time*, *A Round of Golf With Tommy Armour* and *Tommy Armour's ABC's of Golf.* His opus was a book on the history of the PGA of America, published in 1975.

The PGA made him president of National Golf Day and a member of its Advisory Board and Public Relations Committee. The United States Golf Association asked Graffis to serve on its Green Section and Museum committees.

The Graffis resume also included presidencies of the Chicago Press Club, the Headline Club of Chicago, the Indiana Society of Chicago, the Illinois Senior Golf Association and the Golf Writers Association of America, which he cofounded.

For his contributions to golf, Herb Graffis was voted into the World Golf Hall of Fame under the category of "Distinguished Service." Of this honor, the self-effacing Graffis said, "I was voted in by guys who were kind enough to forget that distinguished service means what you had better damn well do, or go broke."

The tributes poured in when Graffis died in 1989 at the age of 95 in Fort Myers, Fla. "He was a friend to all of us," said Ben Hogan. "All of us will miss him. He sure was good for golf," said Sam Snead. Arnold Palmer, who grew up reading *The Greenskeeper Reporter* with his father in Latrobe, Pa., called Graffis, "a humorous man, a great guy, a good friend." *The Fort Myers News Press* called Graffis, "a giant in the world of golf, a writer about golf, a larger-than-life man known and admired by the game's royalty, its courtiers and its spear-carriers."

But perhaps it was Dr. Joseph F. Beditz, Executive Vice President and acting President and CEO of the NGF, who summed up Herb Graffis best. "Herb Graffis's contributions to golf cannot be measured," said Beditz. "No one who ever met Herb will ever forget him. His writing on golf is legendary; his efforts to promote the game and his love for golf will stand as a testimonial for future generations . . . Only death has silenced one of the great voices of our game."

THE GRAFFIS RECORD

Golf Columnist, *Chicago Sun Times*

Founder, National Golf Foundation

Founder, *Golfdom* **Magazine: 1919**

Founder, *Golfing* **Magazine: 1933**

Author, *History of the PGA* **and 3 books with Tommy Armour**

President and Cofounder, Golf Writers Association of America: 1951-1952

Donald Ross

Mention the name Donald Ross to an educated golfer, and it will surely bring good thoughts to mind. That is because Ross, in the words of Jack Nicklaus, designed golf courses that led to positive thinking. "His stamp as an architect was naturalness," Nicklaus said. He was, and still is, considered the Michelangelo of golf.

The Ross touch is on some of this nation's most memorable, and playable, courses. His most famous designs are Pinehurst No. 2, Seminole, Oak Hill and Oakland Hills, but Ross was a man of both quality and quantity. He is credited with 600 designs and redesigns, although some were during his "mail order" era when the demand for his work was so high that he would route courses for property he never saw. Ross would take the topographical maps brought to him, lay out a course on the top, and the club's greenkeeper or engineer would oversee the construction. Ross did, however, oversee work on a good percentage of the courses which bear his name.

Ross was born in Dornoch, Scotland, educated in golf at St. Andrews under Old Tom Morris, and brought to this country in 1899 by a Harvard professor, Robert Wilson. Investing his entire life's savings into the trip to America, Ross walked off the boat in Boston with only $2 in his pocket, but a job was waiting for him, thanks to Wilson, at Oakley Country Club in Watertown, Mass. The following summer he was brought to North Carolina by James Tufts, the man who founded Pinehurst, as the club's professional. Although he had no experience as a golf course architect, Ross was commissioned by Tufts to design Pinehurst's first four courses, and his career skyrocketed to the point where he became one of golf's first celebrities.

Alternating between Boston in the summer and Pinehurst during the winter, Ross won three North and South Opens, two Massachusetts Opens and finished fifth in the 1903 U.S. Open as well as eighth in the 1910 British Open. It was a notable record, but Ross's younger brother, Alex, was the best player in the family, winning the U.S. Open in 1907 in addition to five North and South Opens and six Massachusetts Open titles.

Ross eventually gave up playing and teaching to concentrate on golf course design. Borrowing from what he learned growing up on the links of Dornoch, Ross made the crowned green his trademark. He was a detail man who took great patience to make sure every slope and break met his approval. All his bunkers looked as though they hadn't been built at all, but had be made by the hands of nature. There is a seamless, timeless quality to Donald Ross golf courses that required very little earth-moving to construct.

Pinehurst No. 2 is a perfect example. Water comes into sight on only one hole, and it is not in play. The course is not particularly long, there is little rough, it is almost impossible to lose a golf ball, yet any golfer who goes around close to his or her handicap will have had a good day. Ross spent more time tweaking this layout than any other of his designs, if not for any other reason that Bob Jones selected Alister Mackenzie over him to design Augusta National. He wanted to make No. 2 the No. 1 course in the South, and there are those who believe that Ross succeeded. Having already played host to a PGA Championship, a Ryder Cup and two TOUR Championships, Pinehurst No. 2, Ross's masterpiece, will be the site of the U.S. Open in 1999.

THE ROSS RECORD

North and South Open: 1903, 1905, 1906

Served as an apprentice to Old Tom Morris at St. Andrews in 1899

Designer or redesigner of 600 courses, including Pinehurst No. 2, Seminole, Oakland Hills, Oak Hill, Inverness, Scioto, Skokie, Interlachen.

Sandra Haynie

This is the story of a renaissance woman who had two careers on the LPGA Tour -- one in which she qualified for the Hall of Fame and one in which she came back to remind everyone just how good she really was.

From 1962-75, Sandra Haynie had won 39 tournaments on the LPGA Tour. Two years later, at the age of 34, she left golf. The reasons? An ulcer, brought on by the pressure of competition, and a circulation problem in her left hand, caused by years of hitting golf balls — she began competing in amateur tournaments when she was 12 — that resulted in arthritis. "I'd come out to the course," she said describing those years, "and wish I were someplace else."

So rather than fight, she surrendered, and returned home to Dallas, to find, in her words, "the peaceful center that I knew was somewhere inside me — or ought to be." During that time, she became mentor to Martina Navratilova, managing the tennis great to her first Wimbledon singles victory in 1978. Known as a cerebral golfer, Haynie taught Navratilova the art of winning and in so doing, she became more in control of herself.

Haynie's body recovered, and so did her mind. In 1980, watching Jack Nicklaus win the U.S. Open on television, Haynie wondered what it would feel like to do the same thing. In 1974, she had won the LPGA Championship and the U.S. Women's Open within a few weeks of each other, but she was only 29 at the time, and didn't fully appreciate what it meant.

Now, at 37, she was having thoughts of staging a comeback. "The only question I had was, do I really want to do this all over again?" she said in a 1982 interview with *The New York Times.* "All the traveling, all the pressure of tournaments, being involved in the growing of the women's Tour? Did I want to go through all that stress again? 'Sandra,' I said to myself, 'Are you that crazy?' And the answer was, 'Absolutely.'"

By 1981, she was playing a full schedule on the LPGA Tour again, and her 40th victory came that year, at the Henredon Classic. In 1982, Haynie closed out her career by winning back-to-back tournaments, the Rochester International and the Peter Jackson Classic, which was her fourth career major. She won by making a 10-foot par putt on the 72nd hole to avoid a playoff with Beth Daniel.

Listening to Haynie describe it makes you realize just how strong she was mentally. "I just put my head down and concentrated. I focused on the shot totally," she said. "I thought about my stroke, which had been so good all day. And then I looked at the hole. It looked huge. As soon as I hit the putt, I knew it was good. I didn't even see it go in the hole. I just whooped."

That victory moved Sandra ahead of Patty Berg on the all-time LPGA victory list. Her knee gave out in 1984, and in 1985 she underwent electrode treatment to deaden the sensitivity in her lower back. She became involved with the National Arthritis Foundation. In 1988, she passed the $1 million mark in career earnings, and at that point, there was nothing left to accomplish. This time she did walk away, but on her terms.

THE HAYNIE RECORD

Major Championship Victories 4
  U.S. Women's Open: 1974
  LPGA: 1965, 1974
  Peter Jackson Classic: 1982
LPGA Victories 42
Player of the Year: 1970

Carol Mann

She was literally one of the giants of the game, both on the golf course and for the work she did in the formation of the "modern" Ladies Professional Golf Association. She was a natural leader, winning a U.S. Women's Open, 38 events, and serving as one of the LPGA's most influential presidents. Yes, she was 6-foot-3, and yes, she was self-conscious about her height, but Carol Mann always seemed quite natural in her surroundings, whether it was taking on Kathy Whitworth and Mickey Wright, or selling the ladies' Tour to corporate America. There was a time when she was the LPGA's Mann for all seasons.

In 1968, she won 10 times and the Vare Trophy with a then-record 72.04 scoring average. The next year she won eight times, and was the LPGA's leading money winner. Starting with the Women's Western Open in 1964, and ending with Lawson's Open in 1975, she towered over everybody in the competition except Whitworth. And then it all became too much for her.

Like Whitworth and Sandra Haynie in the late 1970s, she just burned out. "I had made a tremendous effort, and it still wasn't satisfying," Mann told Liz Kahn in her unauthorized history of the LPGA. I said to my father: "Daddy, is this all there is to life? Is this all the accomplishment I can expect? Is this the only kick I'm going to have? Do I have to keep doing this?"

He replied, "No, baby, this isn't all there is."

She read Norman Vincent Peale's *The Power of Positive Thinking*, and did self-hypnosis with Bob Hagge. Unlike Whiteworth and Haynie, Mann could never resurrect her playing career, in part because she was too busy helping to shape and run the ladies' Tour.

Mann was the LPGA's president from Sept. 5, 1975, to May 31, 1976. It was during this time that the LPGA hired marketing genius Ray Volpe as its commissioner. Playing competitive golf had become secondary. "I could barely get to the course in time to tee off; there was so much other activity," she remembers. "By June 1976, I went down the tubes. I was depressed thinking that no one on Tour would say thank you to me for what I had done. Some would, others never would, and 10 years later, players wouldn't give a damn."

Mann was appreciated; she received the Babe Zaharias Award in 1976 and was looked upon as one of the "100 Heroes of American Golf." She was inducted into the LPGA's Hall of Fame in 1977.

Mann didn't develop a golf swing until she was 13 years old, after the family moved to Chicago and took a membership at Olympia Fields C.C. Commuting to tournaments on trains, Mann won the Western Junior and the Chicago Junior in 1958, and the Chicago Women's Amateur in 1960. "I was awkward, shy, without any poise, and I giggled," Mann said.

Mann overcame her insecurities to enjoy one of the most productive careers in women's golf history. She retired at age 40 and began to branch out in different directions. The Women's Sports Foundation made her a trustee and she served as president from 1985-1990. She also formed Carol Mann Golf Services, the first woman-owned and operated course design and management firm. Based in Houston, she started teaching at The Woodlands C.C. and settled into her 50s quite nicely.

"I've walked on the moon," she has said. "I enjoy being a person, and getting old and dying are fine. I never think how people will remember Carol Mann. The mark I made is an intimate satisfaction."

THE MANN RECORD

Major Championship Victories 1
  U.S. Women's Open: 1965
LPGA Tour Victories 38
Vare Trophy: 1968
LPGA Leading Money Winner: 1969
LPGA President, LPGA : 1974, 1975
Babe Zaharias Award: 1976

Billy Casper

Because of an ultra-efficient manner of play and a quiet personality that contrasted with the more dynamic images of his more famous contemporaries, Billy Casper is perhaps the most underrated star in golf history.

Between 1956 and 1975, Casper won 51 times on the PGA TOUR, a figured surpassed by only Snead, Nicklaus, Palmer, Hogan and Nelson. He won two U.S. Opens and a Masters. He was a member of eight Ryder Cup teams, winning more points, 23.5, than any other American player. He won the Vardon Trophy five times, a record matched only by Lee Trevino. He was PGA Player of the Year in 1966 and 1970.

In his prime, however, Casper was overshadowed by Palmer, Nicklaus and Gary Player, who were marketed as The Big Three. But from 1964 to 1970, Casper won 27 U.S. events, eight more than Palmer and Player combined, and four more than Nicklaus.

Casper, of course, did not lack for respect among his peers. "Billy was a killer on the golf course," said Dave Marr. "He just gave you this terrible feeling he was never going to make a mistake, and then of course he'd drive that stake through your heart with that putter. It was a very efficient operation." Said Lee Trevino, "When I came up, I focused on Casper. I figured he was twice as good as me, so I watched how he practiced and decided I would practice three times as much as him."

Casper was born in June 24, 1931, in San Diego, Calif., where sports quickly became the center of his life. "When I was in first grade, the kids called me Fatso," he remembered. "It hurt, but the way I overcame it was to outrun every kid in the class. So I developed a thick skin, and athletics became my way of performing and being accepted." He caddied at the San Diego C.C., and came out of the same junior golf environment that also produced Gene Littler and Mickey Wright. "I didn't really worry about form, and to be honest, I was too lazy to go out there and hit the ball," Casper said. "I would chip and putt or play sand shots. That was the genesis of my short game."

Among the game's greatest winners, Casper was the greatest-putter. He used a pigeon-toed stance and gave the ball a brisk, wristy pop. Casper's self taught swing was distinctive for the way his right foot would slide through impact. Off the tee, it produced a fade that was always in play, and approaches that inevitably finished pin high. Whatever shot Casper was playing, it was executed with supreme touch and feel. "Billy has the greatest pair of hands God ever gave a human being," contends Johnny Miller.

He was also a tremendous competitor. The most enduring memory for those who watched and competed against him in his prime is the serene assurance of the supremely confident athlete who knew he would be at his best when it mattered most. The greatest example of this relentless quality was at the 1966 U.S. Open, where he made up seven strokes on the final nine to tie Arnold Palmer, and then defeated him in a playoff the next day.

But Casper seemed a ghostly figure. At the peak of his powers, Casper got more attention for his allergies, his conversion to Mormonism, his 11 children (six of them adopted) and his offbeat diet of buffalo meat and organically grown vegetables. At first he was hefty, and later lost 70 pounds to drop to 170. When he played, it seemed as if he was in a trance. "It came from my feelings for Hogan," said Casper, who indeed experimented with self-hypnosis. "He seemed to be in this sort of hypnotic state, and I wanted to be just as focused." The public would come to know very little of Billy Casper, making him arguably the best modern golfer who never received his due.

THE CASPER RECORD

Major Championship Victories	3
Masters: 1970	
U.S. Open: 1959, 1966	
PGA TOUR Victories	51
SENIOR PGA TOUR Victories	8
Ryder Cup Teams	9
(20-10-7) 1961, 1963, 1965, 1967, 1969, 1971, 1973, 1975	
Captain:	1979
PGA Player of the Year: 1966, 1970	
Vardon Trophy: 1960, 1963, 1965, 1966, 1968	
Leading Money Winner: 1966, 1968	
Byron Nelson Award: 1966, 1968, 1970	

Harold Hilton

Harold Hilton's place in golf history was literally etched in stone at Apawamis Country Club in Rye, N.Y. Playing the 37th hole of the 1911 U.S. Amateur final against Fred Herreshoff, Hilton hit a spoon (3-wood) that was headed into a rock bed right of the first green. As if guided by the hands of fate, the ball ricocheted onto the putting surface, stunning Herreshoff, who half-topped his approach shot and made bogey. With three British Amateur and two British Open victories to his credit, Hilton two-putted for par, and at 42, become the first foreign-born player to win the U.S. Amateur. At Apawamis, they still call it Hilton's Rock.

The shock waves sent off by Hilton's victory were far-reaching. Herbert Warren Wind described it as "the most discussed single shot ever played in an American tournament." In *The Story of American Golf*, Wind wrote that, "Americans were not at all pleased over the idea that a foreigner had carried one of our championship cups out of the country, and that men who had never cared about golf before now wanted to know the real inside story." Wind used the press as a touchstone, noting that a New York newspaper which identified the Englishman as "Horace H. Hilton" in a story prior to the Amateur, had gotten Hilton's first name right when he won the event.

In Great Britain, Hilton had been famous since well before the turn of the century. In 1892, he won the first Open Championship played over 72 holes. Few amateurs were in the field, and Hilton wasn't sure about traveling from his home at Hoylake to Muirfield, Scotland, until the week of the event. With only one practice round to draw on, Hilton was seven strokes back at the halfway point. He shot 72-74 over the final 36

holes to shoot 305 and win by three strokes. One of the players he defeated was his Royal Liverpool clubmate John Ball, who in 1890 had become the first amateur to win the Open Championship.

Five years later, the Open was played at Hoylake for the first time. Hilton and Ball were among the favorites, but the field of 86 golfers included the "Great Triumverate" of Harry Vardon, James Braid and J.H. Taylor. The tournament came down to the final hole. Hilton had posted 314, and was in the clubhouse, playing billiards, awaiting the outcome. When word came that Braid was playing the 18th, Hilton went out to watch. Braid's cleek shot nearly went in the hole, but the Scotsman missed his birdie putt, and Hilton had won his second Open.

Hilton was a wild-swinger, who regripped the club at the top of his backswing. Although standing only 5 feet, 5 inches, he was a powerful, if unconventional shotmaker. After losing to him in the 1913 Amateur at St. Andrews, Robert Harris once wrote of Hilton: "His cap used to fall from his head at the end of a full swing, as if jerked off, but this did not indicate that his swing was not pure if apparently unduly forceful. He was a small man of powerful physique; it was exhilarating to watch his perky walk between shots. His assiduity was his greatness."

After retiring from competitive golf, Hilton became a writer of popular books on golf and was editor of several golf magazines. In 1923, just as Bob Jones and Walter Hagen were coming on the scene, he addressed the impending takeover by the American golfer; what Hilton failed to point out that the motivation was his victory at Apawamis. It helped shape the course of American golf history.

THE HILTON RECORD

Major Tournament Victories 7
  U.S. Amateur: 1911
  British Amateur: 1900, 1901, 1911, 1913
  British Open: 1892, 1897

Dorothy Campbell Hurd

Dorothy Campbell Hurd was the first woman to dominate international golf. Between 1905 and 1912, she won 10 national championships in America, England, Scotland and Canada. Then, 12 years later, she won the American title once more.

As Dorothy Campbell, and later as Mrs. J.V. Hurd, her count of national amateurs was three U.S., two British, three Scottish and three Canadian. In 1909, she became the first woman to win the U.S. and British Amateurs in the same year.

Dorothy Campbell was born in 1883 in North Berwick, Scotland. The town's famous links, where her paternal grandfather and eight uncles all played, proved her playground. She took her first swing when she was 18 months, and by age five, was playing matches against her older sisters.

Campbell did not evolve into a top player until her late teens, when she changed what had been a half-swing into a full one. In 1905, Campbell won her first Scottish Ladies title. Played at the North Berwick links, more than 4,000 people watched her win the final on the 19th hole. She repeated in 1906 and 1908. The next year, she entered the U.S. Women's Amateur for the first time, and won at the Merion Cricket Club. When she returned to achieve her first victory in the British Women's Amateur Championship at Royal Birkdale, it was an unprecedented double.

In 1910, Campbell moved to Canada and won that country's championship three consecutive years before moving to the United States permanently in 1913. When she won the American title again in 1924, she was 41 years old. She remains the championship's oldest winner, and her 15-year span between victories is also the longest in the event's history.

Hurd advanced women's golf in America by being the first to aim directly at the pin on her approaches instead of just the general vicinity of the green. She had a tremendous short game, which she once said, "is almost second nature to me." A deadly putter, she was even better from just off the green. Her favorite club was a goose-necked mashie she called "Thomas." It was "Thomas" that she gave credit to for her American-British double, for in the semifinal at Birkdale, she used the club to hole out from a dead stymie at a crucial point in the match. In the final of the 1921 North and South championship at Pinehurst, "Thomas" holed two shots.

After her flurry of national titles, Campbell married and her golf career hit a fallow period. When she lost the final of the 1920 U.S. Amateur to Alexa Stirling, it appeared to be her last hurrah. But in 1923, seeing that many women were outdriving her by using a more modern technique, she concluded that her game needed updating.

She changed her swing from a stiff-wristed, sweeping-type motion that produced a straight but short left-to-right shot to a more athletic action in which hand action played an important part. Working with George Sayers, the pro at Merion who was also from North Berwick, she forced herself to switch from the baseball to the Vardon grip. After 10 months of work, Hurd was literally a new player. At the 1924 U.S. Amateur at Rhode Island C.C., she rolled through the field, ultimately defeating Mary K. Browne, the national lawn tennis champion of 1912 and 1913, 7 and 6, in the final.

Although it was Hurd's last championship, she was far from finished as a golfer. In 1926, she set out to surpass the record for fewest putts in 18 holes, 21, which had been set by Walter J. Travis. At the Augusta C.C., Hurd came to the 18th hole with 19 putts, when she holed out from off the green using "Thomas," her famous mashie.

THE HURD RECORD

Major Championships Victories . . . 5
  Womens Amateur: 1909, 1910, 1924
  British Womens Amateur: 1909, 1911
Other Significant Victories
  Scottish Ladies: 1905, 1906, 1908
  Canadian Ladies Open: 1910, 1911, 1912
  U.S. Women's Senior: 1938

Bing Crosby

Throw out Jones and Palmer, and Bing Crosby may be the person most responsible for popularizing the game of golf. Since 1937 the Crosby Clambake—which now carries the heftier title AT&T Pebble Beach National Pro-Am—has been the game's most glamorous event, a four-day party combining glittering Hollywood stars, sweeping ocean vistas and some surprisingly serious golf. "This little tournament is the best advertisement golf has ever had," Crosby once said, and his words still hold true.

Born Harry Lillis Crosby in 1904 in Tacoma, Wash., Crosby first took up the game at 12 as a caddy, dropped it, and started again in 1930 with some fellow cast members in Hollywood during the filming of "The King of Jazz." Although he made his name as a singer, vaudeville performer and silver screen luminary, he would probably prefer to be remembered as a two handicap who competed in both the British and U.S. Amateur championships, a five time club champion at Lakeside Golf Club in Hollywood, and as one of only a few players to have made a hole-in-one on the 16th at Cypress Point.

He conceived his tournament as a friendly little pro-am for his fellow members at Lakeside Golf Club and any stray touring pros who could use some pocket change. The first edition of the Clambake was played at Rancho Santa Fe C.C., in northern San Diego county, where Crosby was also member. He kicked in $3,000 of his own money for the purse, which led inaugural champion Sam Snead to ask if might get his $700 in cash instead of a check. Snead's suspicions notwithstanding, the tournament was a rollicking success, thanks to the merry membership of Lakeside, an entertainment industry enclave in North Hollywood. That first tournament set the precedent for all that followed, as it was as much about partying as it was about golf.

Of course, the competitors were sodden in more ways than one. The first Clambake was played in such a deluge, an on-course bridge was washed out, and this foul weather would also become a hallmark. "One thing about Crosby weather, there's lots of it," the host once said. Relocating to Monterey Peninsula after World War II only made it worse. In 1962, snow postponed the tournament for a day, and 34 years later rain wiped it out altogether.

Still, moving up north was the best thing that ever happened to the Clambake. Rotating among Pebble Beach Golf Links, the Cypress Point Club and Spyglass Hill, the tournament finally had golf courses that could match the star power of the golfers. The climactic final round has always been played at Pebble, helping to establish the course not only as a major championship venue but also the one track that every duffer dreams of playing.

Crosby died in 1977 of a heart attack while on a golf course in Madrid, having just played 18 holes with Spanish professional Manual Pinero. His tournament continued to thrive under the watchful eye of his son Nathaniel, the U.S. Amateur champion in 1981. In recent years it has enjoyed a renaissance thanks in part to Jack Lemmon's increasingly quixotic quest to make the cut and Bill Murray's hilarious antics. Though it no longer carries his name, the Pebble Beach National Pro-Am will always be Bing Crosby's tournament. As he once said, "If I were asked what single thing has given me the most gratification in my long and sometimes pedestrian career, I think I would have to say it is this tournament."

THE CROSBY RECORD

Started Bing Crosby Clambake: 1937

William D. Richardson Award: 1950

Bob Jones Award: 1978

Clifford Roberts

The words used to describe Clifford Roberts were autocratic, mysterious, intimidating, and often, enigmatic. He seemed to rule the Masters Tournament and Augusta National Golf Club from behind an iron curtain, yet those who knew him respected him, and what he did for golf. While Bobby Jones got much of the credit, Cliff Roberts did most of the the work.

They were the good cop and the bad cop, the ying and the yang, working together in creating and administrating two of the game's most significant institutions.

Roberts was the perfect complement to Jones, who was loved and revered, and whose influence made the Masters one of golf's major championships. As approachable as Jones was, Roberts was just the opposite. He worked behind the scenes as an administrator, helping to mold the club's conscience and the tournament's reputation as the best-run golf event in the world.

Herbert Warren Wind provided this description of their chemistry when Roberts died in 1977 at age 84 of a self-inflicted gunshot wound: "Jones imparted to the Masters an atmosphere of golf at its best. He was the perfect host, since it was a true pleasure for him to greet old and new friends and to see that they were made to feel at home. Roberts, on the other hand, was of an extremely reserved disposition. Spare in build and somewhat stonefaced, he said no more on any subject than he had to."

Roberts was a Wall Street financier who came to enjoy the Augusta spa with friends in the 1920s. It was a time when Jones would travel from Atlanta to play golf, and as Augusta regulars, they formed a bond that would result in the construction of America's most famous golf course and tournament. It was Roberts's idea to form a holding company and sold Jones on the idea of a national membership — no more than 30 people from the Augusta area would be allowed to join the club. The initiation fee was set at $350, with dues at $60 a year. Together, they passed over Donald Ross and decided upon Alister Mackenzie as the course architect. They purchased a 365-acre, pre-Civil War indigo plantation that had been turned into Berckman's Nursery, and made it into a golfing landmark.

When illness struck down Jones, Roberts assumed total responsibility over the club and the tournament. It was the unbending manner in which he refused to grant special favors that made the Masters such an efficient operation. "The standards and quality with which he conducted the Masters are unmatched anywhere," said Jack Nicklaus. "All of us in golf appreciate what he has done for the game."

It didn't matter whether it was a member of the media pressing him for tournament attendance figures or a member of the club pushing him on policy. Roberts, as veteran columnist Tom Callahan once wrote, was something of a stone monument.

One year, a member suggested that a mound be put behind a certain green. "Fine, we'll do that," Roberts reportedly said. Several months later the member received a bill for the entire cost of the improvement. Asked in later years if that ever happened, Roberts replied firmly, "I don't remember it."

Roberts instituted such innovations as gallery roping, pairing sheets, course maps, stadium mounding and an elaborate scoring and leaderboard operation.

"Although he was a tough man, he was a person who was truly dedicated to golf and the quality and standards of the game," Arnold Palmer said. "And when you got to know him—as I was fortunate enough to be able to do—you found him to be a very nice and warm person. I liked and admired him very much."

THE ROBERTS RECORD

Co-Founder, Augusta National Golf Club: 1934

Chairman, Masters Tournament

Louise Suggs

"She was bound to be a winner," Ben Hogan once said of Louise Suggs. "And, she was."

No truer words have been spoken in describing the first inductee into the LPGA Hall of Fame. Suggs won a U.S. Amateur, a British Amateur, two U.S. Women's Opens, an LPGA Championship and a Vare Trophy. In all, she won 50 tournaments, including eight major championships.

Overshadowed only by the popularity of Babe Zaharias, Suggs won often, and in record-setting ways. In the 1949 Women's Open, she set the 72-hole scoring record of 291 and won by 14 strokes over Zaharias, which stood as an LPGA record until Cindy Mackey won by 14 strokes in the 1986 MasterCard International. Four years later, Suggs broke her own LPGA scoring record by shooting 288 to win the 1953 Tampa Open at Palma Ceia.

In the foreword to Suggs's book, *Par Golf for Women*, Hogan wrote: "If I were to single out one woman in the world today as a model for any other woman aspiring to ideal golf form it would be Miss Suggs. Her swing combines all the desirable elements of efficiency, timing and coordination. It appears to be completely effortless. Yes, despite her slight build, she is consistently as long off the tee and through the fairway as any of her feminine contemporaries in competitive golf. And no one is 'right down the middle' any more than this sweet-swinging Georgia miss."

Born in Atlanta, Suggs had the benefit of growing up in a golf environment (her father, John, a former pitcher with the New York Yankees and Atlanta Crackers, owned and managed a golf course.) She won the Georgia State Amateur in 1940 and 1942, the Southern Amateur twice, the Western Amateur twice, and the North and South three times. She won the Titleholders, which was then considered a major championship, as an amateur in 1946 and followed that with the U.S. and British Amateurs in 1947 and 1948, respectively.

With nothing left to accomplish on the amateur level, Suggs turned pro and made her first victory the record-setting performance over Zaharias in the Women's Open. It was an especially sweet victory for Suggs, who resented the tremendous publicity given to Babe. It was because of Babe, however, that sponsors became interested in ladies' golf, and with the help of golf promoter Fred Corcoran, Suggs, Zaharias, Patty Berg, Marilynn Smith, Betty Jameson helped found the LPGA in 1950. Berg was the first president, and she was succeeded by Suggs from 1955-1957.

Sadly, Suggs's career came to an end over a matter of principle. In 1962, she was fined $25 for failing to play in event in Milwaukee to which she had committed. Feeling wronged, she never played a full schedule again. "She was at the height of her career and in her prime when she quit," said Betsy Rawls, who was president of the LPGA at the time. "It was hard for me to understand that kind of thinking. I would have paid for her myself, although the money was nothing to Louise. I forever regretted it for her, and I thought it was one of the saddest things in the LPGA history."

THE SUGGS RECORD

Major Championship Victories. . . 13
  U.S. Women's Amateur: 1947
  British Women's Amateur: 1948
  U.S. Women's Open: 1949, 1952
  Women's Western Open: 1946, 1947, 1949, 1953
  LPGA: 1957
  Titleholders: 1947, 1954, 1956, 1959
LPGA Tour Victories 50
Curtis Cup Teams 1
  (0-1-1) 1948
Vare Trophy: 1957
Leading Money Winner: 1953, 1960
LPGA President: 3 times

Walter Travis

There has not been a golfer who played so well after starting so late in life as Walter J. Travis. Here was a man who didn't hit his first golf ball until he was 35, yet one month later he won his first tournament and two years later he reached the semifinals of the U.S. Amateur. Within four years of picking up a club for the first time, Travis won the first of three National Amateurs. He also was the first American citizen to win the British Amateur, and ended his career, at age 53, by winning the prestigious Metropolitan Amateur in New York.

Weighing no more than 140 pounds, with small hands and slender wrists, Travis relied on cunning and his short game to excel at match play. He made up for a lack in size by simply outputting and outworking everybody. In his autobiography, first printed in *The American Golfer*, which he founded in 1908, Travis explained how he became a "golf fiend."

"I am not aware of ever having possessed any physical advantages that enabled me to climb the ladder as I did in such a comparatively short space of time," Travis wrote. "What success I managed to achieve was primarily due to an intense love of the game, a devotion which made practice not a drudgery but a pleasure. 'Genius,' I think it was Carlyle, who said, 'is the capacity of taking infinite pains.' I practiced at every opportunity."

Born in Australia, Travis came in the United States and made a substantial income in the hardware business. He played cricket and lawn tennis as a young man, without much success, and became hooked on golf after a visit to England in 1896. His most cherished trophy was the pewter tankard won in the first handicap competition at the Oakland Golf Club of Bayside, L.I. His first U.S. Amateur victory came in 1900 at Garden City Golf Club on Long Island, and his name was engraved on the Havemeyer

Trophy again in 1901 and 1903.

In 1902, he set a U.S. Open record by shooting 75-74–149 for the final two rounds. The second-place finish to Laurie Auchterlonie was the highest by an amateur in the Open, and rather than collect the $100 price, Travis asked the USGA to reserve $75 for a trophy. The remaining $25 was given to his playing companion, Alex Smith, whom Travis thought displayed "thoroughly sportsmanlike spirit throughout."

Two years later, Travis traveled to Royal St. George's at Sandwich, England, for the British Amateur. On his way to the final, he defeated two of Britain's best golfers in Harold Hilton and Horace Hutchinson. The final was a relative breeze, as he defeated Ted Blackwell to win the famous cup. It was not until 1926 that another American could come along and win the British Amateur, and those who tried included Jones, Chick Evans, Jerry Travers and Francis Ouimet.

Travis thrived in match play because he was mentally stronger than most of his opponents. "Always be on the aggressive," Travis wrote in *The American Golfer*. "Act as if you are quite sure of yourself and never give an opponent the psychological advantage of imagining you are the least afraid of him. Many a man is beaten before he starts by admitting to himself the other's fancied superiority and unconsciously conveying it in his general bearing. It only gives the opponent that slight encouragement which enables him to pull out a winner in a tight match."

In his later years, Travis would hang out on the practice green at Garden City G.C., challenging the members to a putting contest. The stakes were usually a cigar, and it was rare when Travis had to buy. He died in 1927, at age 65, without any regrets. "Full as my cup has been," he said, "I shall never cease to regret the many prior years which were wasted."

THE TRAVIS RECORD

Major Championship Victories 4
U.S. Amateur: 1900, 1901, 1903
British Amateur: 1904

Founder, *The American Golfer* Magazine: 1908

Lawson Little

In the long history of golf there have been three instances of sustained brilliance. Two are immediately obvious—Bobby Jones's Grand Slam, and Ben Hogan's magical 1953 campaign. Although it is rarely remembered, Lawson Little may have topped them both.

In 1934 and 1935 Little became the first golfer to sweep the British and American Amateur Championships in consecutive years, two "Little Slams" as the pundits of the day referred to them. During his phenomenal run, Little won 32 consecutive matches on both sides of the Atlantic with an overpowering game built on booming drives and brooding intensity. It is a testament to Little's awesome dominance that he followed with a professional career that included seven victories and a U.S. Open title, and it was considered an failure. Wrote Charles Price, "Lawson Little was the greatest match player in the history of golf."

Born in Newport, R.I. in 1910, and raised in Northern California, Little burst onto the scene at Pebble Beach in the 1929 U.S. Amateur, when he defeated Johnny Goodman the day after Goodman had electrified the golf world by beating the seemingly unbeatable Bobby Jones. Five years later, at the British Amateur at Prestwick, the 24–year–old with the senatorial mane of dark, wavy hair, realized his potential. He barely broke a sweat in winning his seven consecutive matches, and in the final, he gave the Scot James Wallace a spanking of legendary proportions. Little shot an unofficial 66 in the morning, five better than course record, and was 12-up by lunchtime. In the afternoon he birdied three of the first five holes and put Wallace out of his misery, 14 & 13. In the 23 holes Little had 12 3s on his card.

Nicknamed "Cannonball," and often described as "bullnecked" and "barrel-chested," the 200 pound Little generated tremendous power despite standing only 5'9". He liked to play the ball far back off his right leg and hit an exaggerated hook. At the 1934 U.S. Amateur at The Country Club, Little

again overpowered the field, taking six 18-hole matches and a pair at 36 holes including the final which Spec Goldman succumbed, 8 & 7. Harold Hilton and Bobby Jones were (and are) the only other golfers to hold the British and American amateur titles simultaneously.

For all his strength, Little had an expert short game. He used a variety of clubs from around the green, and in fact often carried as many seven wedges among his 26 clubs, an excess which in 1938 prompted the USGA to institute the 14 club limit.

As Little's reputation as a merciless competitor continued to mushroom, so too did the estimation that he was a surly and unlikable champion. Having grown up the son of a colonel in Army Medical Corps, bouncing from base to base across the United States and China, Little was admittedly withdrawn, but he attributed his on-course demeanor to an unparalleled concentration.

"The man who doesn't plan out every shot to the very top of his capacity for thought can't attain championship form," he said. Little also believed "Winners hit their bad shots best."

In the spring of 1935, Little went to St. Annes to defend his British Amateur title, and he was lucky not to lose his first match. Despite a shaky 80, he stole the match on the 18th green, and from there he took the title without incident. Little's inexorable march into the record books was completed at the Cleveland C.C.

Little turned pro shortly thereafter, and his mediocre record was often attributed to a lack of desire that came from being among the first pros with significant endorsement money. When he defeated Gene Sarazen in a playoff to win the 1940 U.S. Open, it was a reminder of what his talents once were. With the advent of World War II, Little lost direction as the major championships were cancelled, and he became more interested in the stock market than in competitive golf. "He never practiced," said Masters and PGA Champion Jack Burke, Jr. "Little either had it that week or he didn't. But when he did have it, it was lights out."

THE LITTLE RECORD

Major Championship Victories 5
  U.S. Amateur: 1934, 1935
  British Amateur: 1934, 1935
  U.S. Open: 1940
Other Significant Victories
  Canadian Open: 1936
  Los Angeles Open: 1940
  Texas Open: 1941
Walker Cup Teams 1
  (2-0-0) 1934

Henry Cotton

"Maestro."

There was a style and substance about Henry Cotton that made him not only unique, but a British national hero. He was much more than just a three-time British Open champion. He also championed the cause of British golf professionals seeking a higher ground in their country's society, and became a patriarch of the European Golf Tour. Described as witty, handsome, intelligent, urbane and a non-conformist, Cotton authored 10 books, designed golf courses and was the most respected and prolific British instructor of his era. His philosophy was simple: "To be a champion, you must act like one."

Cotton was born Jan. 26, 1907, at Holmes Chapel in Cheshire, England. He left private school at age 16 in a dispute with his cricket coach and set out to learn the trade of golf on his own terms. This meant dressing smartly but shunning the traditional jacket and tie, and behaving properly, but never subserviently. Encouraged by Harry Vardon, James Braid and J.H. Taylor, Cotton took his first head professional job three years later, but soon moved to the Waterloo Club in Brussels, where he was treated as an equal.

Cotton's devotion to practice was almost maniacle, for he believed the only secrets to becoming a champion golfer were hard work and strong hands. For hours upon hours, Cotton was known to hit balls from thick rough until his hands blistered and bled. It was an obsession that paid off in the 1934 Open at Royal St. George's. With opening rounds of 67-65—132, Cotton set two scoring records and opened a lead that was insurmountable. Even with a 79 in the final round, Cotton was able to win by five strokes and end a run of overseas victors that had lasted since Arthur Havers triumph in 1923.

Cotton's second British Open triumph came three years later, at Carnoustie, where his final round of 71, shot in a downpour, was considered every bit as good as his record 65. That gave Cotton a two-stroke victory against a field that included every member of a United States Ryder Cup team captained by Walter Hagen that included Gene Sarazen, Byron Nelson, Sam Snead, Ralph Guldahl, Denny Shute and Henry Picard.

It was his third Open Championship, at Muirfield in 1948, that completed Henry Cotton's transformation from the anti-establishment rebel to a national sporting legend and celebrity. Now 41, and robbed of his prime by World War II, Cotton shot a course record 66 in the second round that was witnessed by King George VI. It was the only time a reigning monarch had been present at the Open.

In addition to those popular victories, Cotton also won three British Match Play Championships and nine national championships on the continent of Europe. He played for his country in three Ryder Cup matches and twice captained the British team, but most of his time after the 1948 British Open at Muirfield was dedicated to instruction, designing golf courses and giving back to the game that had given so much to him. Whether it was giving no-cost instruction to junior golfers through the Golf Foundation, or doing exhibitions to raise money for the Red Cross, Henry Cotton was as hard-working and devoted as he had been about learning how to swing a golf club. For this, he was honored with a Knighthood, and on New Year's Day of 1988, just one week after his death, Henry Cotton MBE officially became Sir Henry Cotton, Knight Commander of the Most Honourable Order of St. Michael and St. George.

THE COTTON RECORD

Major Championship Victories 3
  British Open: 1934, 1937, 1948
European Tour Victories: 30
Other Significant Victories
  British Professional Match Play:
    1932, 1940, 1946
  Belgian Open: 1930, 1934, 1938
  Italian Open: 1936
  German Open: 1937, 1939
  French Open: 1946, 1947
Ryder Cup Teams 4
  (2-4-0) 1929, 1937, 1947
  Captain 1947, 1953

Lee Trevino

All golfers are self made, but the man who made the most out of what he started with has to be Lee Trevino.

Trevino rose from a three-room shack with no plumbing in east Dallas to become one of the most consistent shotmakers the game has ever seen. Through an agile mind, a tremendous work ethic and a sense of moment that belongs to the natural performer, Trevino carved a way to the top that is unlike any other in golf history.

Starting as a caddy, and coming up through the ranks of driving ranges, military golf and hustling, Trevino burst into big-time professional golf full blown. He was a squat 5-foot-7, 180-pound ball of fire whose rapid wit made players and gallery laugh, but whose game commanded their respect. In June 1968, the still unknown 28-year-old won the U.S. Open at Oak Hill with a record-tying score of 69-68-69-69—275.

Three years later, Trevino won his second U.S. Open, this time at Merion in a classic 18-hole playoff with Jack Nicklaus. Within 20 days he added the Canadian Open and the British Open at Royal Birkdale, completing an unprecedented international sweep. The next year he won the British Open again, this time at Muirfield. His final two major championships would come in the PGA, first at Tanglewood in 1974, and finally at Shoal Creek in 1984.

Trevino was born on Dec. 8, 1939, in Garland, Texas. Reared by his mother and maternal grandfather, a gravedigger, he never knew his father. As a boy, Trevino was in the cotton fields working by the time he was five. "I thought hard work was just how life was," he said. His family's home was 100 yards from the seventh fairway of the Dallas Athletic Club, and by the time Trevino was eight, he was caddying. "That's where I learned my killer instinct, playing games with the caddies and betting everything I had earned that day," he wrote. He quit school in eighth grade to work on a driving range, where he would hit hundreds of balls a day.

The first complete round he ever played was at the age of 15, when he shot a 77 at a junior tournament. At 17, he joined the Marines and further honed his game. When he got out, he played in money games around Dallas and El Paso, one of which included his hitting the ball around a par-3 course with a Dr. Pepper bottle. "You don't know what pressure is until you play for five bucks with only two in your pocket," he said.

A turning point in his career came when he played at Shady Oaks in Fort Worth and saw Ben Hogan on the practice range. From that day on, Trevino honed a fade that would make him one of the most accurate players the game has ever seen. Sometimes he would yell, "Don't move, hole!" when he'd hit an iron at the pin.

Trevino did it with a strong grip, stood with his body aligned well left of his target, and essentially shoved the ball outward with a strong blocking action of his left side. The British writer Leonard Crawley called it "an agrarian method," but perhaps no one has ever hit the ball as consistently solid. Trevino said, "Who knows, maybe my method is best," he once said. On and around the greens, Trevino was both deft and opportunistic.

Although he was an instant success when he joined the TOUR, Trevino suffered plenty of hard times. In 1975, he was nearly killed when he was hit by lightning during the Western Open, and suffered severe back problems. He also lost two fortunes due to bad investments.

But Trevino called on the resiliency born of his beginnings. In 1980, he had one of his best years, winning the Vardon Trophy for the fifth time. His PGA victory at Shoal Creek was his crowning achievement. In all, he won 27 times on the regular TOUR. Later, he would surpass that total on the SENIOR TOUR.

"I've always had a tremendous amount of confidence in Lee Trevino," he said. "But I've always paid the price."

THE TREVINO RECORD

Major Championship Victories . . . 6
  U.S. Open: 1968, 1971
  British Open: 1971, 1972
  PGA Championship: 1974, 1984

PGA TOUR Victories 27

SENIOR PGA TOUR Victories . . 28

Ryder Cup Teams 7
  (17-7-6) 1969, 1971, 1973,
                 1975, 1979, 1981
  Captain 1985

Vardon Trophy: 1970, 1974, 1980

Ralph Guldahl

Ralph Guldahl stands alone in golf history as the best player ever to suddenly and completely lose his game. Guldahl was born the same year as Ben Hogan, Sam Snead and Byron Nelson, and he shot to the top more quickly than any of them. In fact, during a dazzling stretch from 1936 to 1939, Guldahl was the brightest star in golf, winning two U.S. Opens, a Masters, and three straight Western Opens. And then, mysteriously, he never won again.

Born in 1912 in Dallas, Texas, the precocious Guldahl joined the pro golf tour in the early 1930's, winning the 1932 Phoenix Open. In the final round of the 1933 U.S. Open at the North Shore G.C. outside Chicago, the tall 20 year old picked up nine strokes in 11 holes on Johnny Goodman, and on the 72nd hole needed only a four footer to force a playoff. He missed it, and essentially gave up competition for nearly three years.

Guldahl went home to Dallas and became a used car salesman until he was asked to lay out a nine hole course in Kilgore, Texas. The project inspired Guldahl to take up the game again. He began practicing, and on the advice of doctors caring for his sickly son, moved his family to the California desert. In 1936, a rededicated Guldahl finished eighth in the U.S. Open, and a few weeks later won his first Western Open.

The 1937 season was his best. Guldahl won the Western again, as well as the U.S. Open at Oakland Hills, where he closed with a 69 for a total of 281 that stood as the championship record until 1948. He would have had three major titles but for an incredible reversal at the Masters. Guldahl was four strokes up with only seven to play, but he hit into the water on both the 12th and 13th holes to score a 5 and 6. On the same holes, Byron Nelson scored a 2 and a 3 to blow by Guldahl and win by two.

He finished second in the Masters again in 1938, but eased the sting of that disappointment by becoming the only golfer to win both the Western and the U.S. Open in consecutive years. The latter victory was achieved by six strokes at Cherry Hills in Denver, where Guldahl became the last U.S. Open champion to win the title wearing a necktie. Finally, in 1939, Guldahl got his green jacket in the most stirring performance of his career. With Snead in the clubhouse with a record score of 280, Guldahl fired a 33 on the Augusta National's back nine, highlighted by a 3-wood second to the par 5 13th that finished six feet from the hole and led to a eagle. That scoring record would stand until Ben Hogan shattered it in 1953.

Guldahl in his prime was a golfer with an impressive arsenal. Though his fast and quirky swing produced only marginal power, Guldahl was straight and uncanny in controlling the distance of his approaches. "When Ralph was at his peak," said Snead, "his clubhead came back on the line and went through on the line as near perfect as anyone I've ever seen." He was a deadly lag putter, and perhaps most importantly, had an imperturbable manner. Guldahl moved through his rounds slowly and devoid of emotion, his only distinguishing on course gesture a habit of taking out a comb and running it through his thick black hair. "If Guldahl gave someone a blood transfusion, the patient would freeze to death," said Snead.

But Guldahl admitted that "behind my so called poker face, I'm burning up." Somehow, beginning in the 1940 season, we went from being the man to beat to a beaten man. Whether it was due to the rigors of competition, lack of desire or the vagaries of his swing remains a mystery. One theory maintains that Guldahl lost his game after working on a golf instruction book, which forced him to think about swing mechanics for the first time in his life. Guldahl left the TOUR in 1942, and except for a brief return in 1949, never played it again. But there was no denying Guldahl's brilliance — while it lasted.

THE GULDAHL RECORD

Major Championship Victories 3
  Masters: 1939
  U.S. Open: 1937, 1938
Other Significant Victories
  Western Open: 1936, 1937
PGA TOUR Victories 16
Ryder Cup Team 1
  (2-0-0) 1937

USGA

Julius Boros

If any one player personified the combination of effortless ease, flawless technique and hidden competitive fire, it was Julius Boros.

Everything about the phlegmatic former accountant conveyed relaxation and imperturbality. But when an opportunity to win a championship was on the line, few converted as efficiently or briskly as Boros.

Boros never took a practice swing, and didn't tarry on the greens. "Julius wasn't the kind of man who bent over too much," said Dave Marr with his trademark pith. "He was slowest and fastest," wrote editor Jerry Tarde. "Slowest walking to ball and fastest once he got to it."

Although he did not turn professional until the age of 29, and despite suffering from physical maladies all his life, Boros put together a career that was remarkable for its consistency, longevity and brilliance. He won 18 times between 1952 and 1968, including three major championships. He was PGA Player of the Year in 1952 and 1963, led the money list in 1952 and 1955, and played on four Ryder Cup teams.

His first victory was the 1952 U.S. Open, which he won by four at the Northwood C.C. in Dallas. He won the championship again 1963 at Brookline, birdieing two of the last three holes to get into a playoff with Arnold Palmer and Jackie Cupit, and defeating them with a flawless 70 in the playoff. It made him, at 43, the oldest winner of the championship since Ted Ray. Then in 1968, Boros won the PGA Championship in San Antonio by again defeating Palmer down stretch and, at 48, became the oldest ever winner of a major.

Besides majors, Boros had a way of winning big money events. He won the World Championship of Golf in 1952 and 1955 when the first prize was an astronomical $50,000. His last victory was the 1968 Westchester Classic, which then had the biggest first prize in golf at $50,000. In 1975, the 55-year-old Boros came within a whisker of becoming the oldest winner ever of a PGA TOUR event, losing a

sudden death playoff to Gene Littler at Westchester. Asked when he was going to retire, Boros answered, "Retire to what? I'm already a golfer and a fisherman. I have nothing to retire to."

The son of Hungarian immigrants, Boros was born March 3, 1920, in Fairfield, Conn. A big man at 6 feet and considerably more than 200 pounds, he had a nonchalant bearing that earned him the nickname "Moose." He learned to take things even easier learning during his military stint that he had a bad heart. Despite his apparent imperturbability, he admitted, "I was as apprehensive as the next guy in a tight situation. It felt like razor blades in my stomach."

The biggest reason Boros was able to last so long was that his technique was so free of strain and technically correct. Boros's motto was "swing easy, hit hard," and he could produce plenty of power. Yet the overall effect was one of grace and control, fairways and greens. "Julius Boros is all hands and wrists, like a man dusting the furniture," said 1964 British Open Champion Tony Lema. His iron shots in particular landed with unique softness, as if by parachute. He was also the master of the sand wedge, particularly out of deep rough around the green, his soft, slow swing feathering the ball with uncanny touch.

It all reflected itself in his success at the championship that is most about control, the U.S. Open. Boros finished in the top five of the U.S. Open nine times between 1951 and 1965. And as late as 1973, he was tied for the lead after 62 holes before finishing tied for 7th.

Boros won the 1977 PGA Seniors Championship, and played a key role in the launch of the SENIOR TOUR by making the final birdie putt on the sixth extra hole of sudden death that gave partner Roberto DeVicenzo and him victory over Tommy Bolt and Art Wall in the 1979 Legends of Golf. Boros died on a golf course near his home in Florida on May 28, 1994. His son, Guy, won the 1996 Greater Vancouver Open, making the Boroses one of only three father-son tandems to have won on the PGA TOUR.

THE BOROS RECORD

Major Championship Victories . . . 3
  U.S. Open: 1952, 1963
  PGA: 1968
Other Significant Victories
  PGA Seniors: 1971, 1977
PGA TOUR Victories 18
Ryder Cup Teams 4
  (9-3-4). . . 1959, 1963, 1965, 1967
Leading Money Winner: 1952, 1955
PGA Player of the Year: 1952, 1963

Kathy Whitworth

It is one of the most famous records in golf: 88 victories over a span of 23 years, an average of 3.8 victories per season starting with the Kelly Girl Open in 1962 and ending with the United Virginia Bank Classic in 1985. In those three decades, Kathrynne Ann Whitworth surpassed the victory totals of Mickey Wright (82) and Sam Snead (84) to lodge herself atop the category of Most Tournament Victories By a Professional, Man or Woman.

Whitworth did this with what she considered average talent. "I never had a golf swing," she said. But did she have staying power. From 1965-1973 she was leading money winner eight times, second on the money list twice and third once. In that span, she won the Vare Trophy and Player of the Year honors seven times each.

With all that success, it still took her until 1981 to become the first woman in golf to earn $1 million. Fifteen years later, Karrie Webb became the first woman to accomplish that feat in one year, and she did so with four victories and 12 top-five finishes. Whitworth had eight victories in 1963, eight victories in 1965 and 11 victories in 1968, and in none of these years did she make more than $50,000.

Whit passed the seven-figure threshold at the U.S. Women's Open, the one major championship that eluded her. "I would have swapped being the first to make a million for winning the Open, but it was a consolation which took some of the sting out of not winning."

Born in Monahans, Texas, Whitworth grew up in Jal, N.M., where her father owned a hardware store. She got her first set of clubs from her grandmother, and started playing golf at 15. Two years later Whitworth won the first of two consecutive New Mexico State Amateur titles.

Her start on the LPGA Tour was less than aus-picious. She played 26 events as a rookie, and made less than $1,300. After playing so poorly, Whitworth considered quitting, but a visit to Harvey Penick convinced her to keep going. Self-conscious and shy, Whitworth was adopted by Wright, Betsy Rawls, Gloria Armstrong and Jackie Pung. She soon gained confidence in herself, and her ability.

"When I won eight tournaments in 1963, I was living on a high," Whitworth said. "I got in a winning syndrome. I played really well, and it came easily. You don't think you're that great, but you're in the groove with good concentration. Nothing bothers you. . ."

Whitworth qualified for the LPGA Hall of Fame in 1975, but the stress of playing at such a high level for so long eventually took its toll. She described the 1974 and 1975 seasons as "traumatic," and in the late 1970s, her game deteriorated. Only the pursuit of the $1 million barrier and the records of Wright and Snead kept her going.

Victory No. 82 came in the 1981 Kemper Open. She passed Wright the next year with a victory at the Lady Michelob. Snead's record fell in 1983, when she made a 40-foot putt on the 72nd hole of the Kemper Open. With one last push, she won three times in 1984 and again the following season. At that point, she assumed responsibility as the LPGA's vice president, and ultimately its president.

"I don't think about the legacy of 88 tournaments—I did it because I wanted to win, not to set a record or a goal that no one else could surpass," she said. "I'm not some great oddity. I was just fortunate to be so successful. What I did in being a better player does not make me a better person. When I'm asked how I would like to be remembered, I feel that if people remember me at all, it will be good enough."

THE WHITWORTH RECORD

Major Championship Victories . . . 6
LPGA: 1967, 1971, 1975
Titleholders: 1965, 1966
Women's Western Open: 1967

Total LPGA Victories 88

Player of the Year: 1966, 1967, 1968, 1969, 1971, 1972, 1973

Vare Trophy: 1965, 1966, 1967, 1969, 1970, 1971, 1972,

Leading Money Winner: 1965, 1966, 1967, 1968, 1970, 1971, 1972, 1973

Richardson Award: 1985

Bob Hope

Bob Hope is not the greatest golfer who's ever played the game, but he might be the most enthusiastic. Since the 1920's he has been one of the sport's great ambassadors. As he traversed the globe entertaining both black-tie audiences and battalions of scruffy soldiers, Hope made a second career of teeing it up with Presidents, Princes and the King - in fact he teamed with Arnold Palmer to win the pro-am portion of the Palm Springs Desert Classic in 1962. Three years later Hope took the reigns of that tournament and it has borne his name ever since. As the host of this sprawling party Hope has been a constant reminder that golf is meant to be enjoyed, his own glib observations notwithstanding.

"It's wonderful how you can start out with three strangers in the morning, play 18 holes, and by the time the day is over you have three solid enemies," Hope once said.

Of course, he has made few enemies on the golf course, in no small part because of his contagious zest for the game. Even though his mansion in Studio City, Calif. was only eight blocks from Lakeside Country Club - which was also home to another of golf's patron saints, Bing Crosby - Hope installed his own kidney shaped green guarded by a pair of bunkers, with three different sets of tees. Back in the old days it was common for houseguests to repair to the back terrace for cocktails and wedges (another set of tees was 140 yards out and mandated a carry over the swimming pool.)

Hope was welcome in almost any foursome. He was a frequent foil for President Eisenhower and a close friend of Ben Hogan, and they supplied many of the countless anecdotes is his ode to the game, *Confessions of a Hooker*. Though he has always liked to poor-mouth his abilities, Hope could actually play a little. He was a four handicap "for about twenty minutes" in his youth, and even teed it up at the 1950 British Open at Troon.

If the Bob Hope Desert Classic lacked the celestial field of the Crosby Clambake, it more than made up for it with perfect weather and the enveloping presence of Hope, a peerless master of ceremonies. Along with his sometimes caddie Phyllis Diller, who usually toted Band-Aids and a hip flask to mitigate any potential disaster, Hope oversaw a pro-am that was at least as much about the ams as the pros. Played on four courses over five days to accommodate the biggest possible field, the Classic remains a tribute to all golfers, from the sublime to the ridiculous. Even though he's pushing 90 Hope still swats the ceremonial first ball. This ardor brings to mind a story Jack Benny used to love to tell.

He encountered Hope one afternoon limping off a course in Palm Springs, moaning about how badly he was playing. Benny went through a whole litany of excuses on Hope's behalf, concluding that with his busy schedule he couldn't possibly play enough golf to keep his game in shape.

"You damn fool," Hope snarled, "I play every day."

THE HOPE RECORD

Started the Bob Hope Tournament:
1960

G. Ravielli

Jimmy Demaret

The impact Jimmy Demaret had on the game of golf was measured by more than his three Masters victories, his impeccable Ryder Cup record and his 44 tournament victories around the world. Jimmy Demaret was golf's first show biz star. He was the reason, some said, that Bing Crosby invented the pro-am. He could sing, he could tell jokes, and for a while, it wasn't a party or a golf tournament unless Demaret was on the premises. He could outdress, outquip and outplay just about everybody in an era that included Ben Hogan, Sam Snead and Byron Nelson.

In the same sentence, Grantland Rice called him the "singing Texan" and the "swinging Texan." Jackie Burke, Jr., once said that Jimmy Demaret "was a jet-setter before there were jets." Herbert Warren Wind referred to him as "The Wardrobe" for fashion statements that singlehandedly put golf clothing on the cutting edge of garish. According to Dan Jenkins, Demaret wore lavender, gold, pink, orange, red and aqua slacks, and yellow, emerald, maroon, plaid, checked, striped and polka-dot sportcoats. He gave shoe factories a swatch from his pants and had matching saddle oxfords made. As Demaret said, "If you're going to be in the limelight, you might as well dress like it."

He was a master of one liners. After a bumpy flight to Japan to play in the World Cup, Demaret got off the plane and said, "Hey, Lindbergh got eight days of confetti for less than this." When it snowed at Pebble Beach in the 1962 Crosby, Demaret piped, "Geez, I know I was drinking last night, but how did I get to Squaw Valley?" And it was Demaret who first said, "Golf and sex are about the only things you can enjoy without being good at them." Bob Hope once called him the funniest amateur comedians in the world.

Demaret was one of the great professional golfers. A stoutly built man with thick arms, he used an elegant wristy swing that shot out low fades with minimal effort. "He was the most underrated golfer in history," said Hogan. "This man played shots I hadn't dreamed of. I learned them. But it was Jimmy who showed them to me first. He was the best wind player I've ever seen in my life."

Born in Houston in 1910, the fifth of nine children, Demaret grew up caddying on sand greens and playing barefoot until he was 15. His father was a carpenter-painter — the source, Demaret said, of his lifelong passion for mixing and matching bright colors. At age 17, he was hired by Jackie Burke, Sr, as an assistant pro at River Oaks in Houston. His first job was to babysit the toddler who would one day be his partner in forming Champions Golf Club, Jackie Burke, Jr. After a brief stint on the pro circuit, Demaret alternated between competitive golf and night club singing before playing the TOUR full time in 1938. In 1940 he won six consecutive tournaments including the Masters. He won six more and the Masters again in 1947, his best year, when he also led the money list and won the Vardon Trophy. In 1950, he won his third Masters and at the presentation grabbed the microphone and began singing, "Do You Know How Lucky You Are."

In all, Demaret won 31 official events between 1938 and 1957, a year in which he won three events at age 47. He was one of the best players never to have won the U.S. Open, finishing two strokes back in 1946 and 1948, and only a stroke out of a playoff in 1957. In three Ryder Cups between 1947 and 1951, his record was 5-0. Along with Gene Sarazen, he was the host on one of the first television golf shows, "Shell's Wonderful World of Golf."

Demaret admitted he would have won more tournaments if he hadn't been so busy enjoying himself. When he died in 1983, golf lost more than just another great champion. It lost a great deal of its charm. "He loves golf," Henry Cotton once said of Demaret, "but no more than a good time."

THE DEMARET RECORD

Major Championship Victories . . . 3
 The Masters: 1940, 1947, 1950

PGA TOUR Victories 31

Ryder Cup Teams 3
 (5-0-0) 1947, 1949, 1951

Vardon Trophy: 1947

Leading Money Winner: 1947

JoAnne Carner

First, she was known as "The Great Gundy." Then, "Big Momma."

She loved match play, showboating to the galleries, riding motorcycles and partying in the clubhouse with the members after her rounds. As JoAnne Gunderson, and later JoAnne Carner, she dominated women's golf — and nobody had more fun dominating than she did. There was a little Babe Ruth in her, a little Babe Zaharias, a little Walter Hagen and a little Shelly Winters, too. It made for some package.

"The ground shakes when she hits it," Sandra Palmer once said, and with that statement the LPGA had a different type of folk hero to package with the glamour of Jan Stephenson and the youthful innocence of Nancy Lopez. While the youngsters were selling the ladies' Tour, Carner was going back to her Gulfstream motor home, where her husband, Don, had prepared dinner and found a stream where the fish were just waiting to take their lures. "I play better golf living in our trailer," Carner said, and for a long while, nobody played it better.

As an amateur golfer, Gunderson was the historic equal with Zaharias and Glenna Collet Vare. Born in Kirkland, Wash., she came out of the Pacific Northwest and won the U.S. Girls' Junior title in 1956. One month later, she lost in the final of the Women's Amateur to Marlene Stewart to begin a 13-year run where she either won the national title or finished second seven times. Four of her five championship finals were blowout victories, but in 1966, it took Carner 42 holes to defeat the then-married Marlene Stewart Streit. It was the longest final match in U.S. Women's Amateur history.

Only Vare, with six, has more U.S. Women's Amateur titles. Carner won her first at age 18 and her last at age 29. It wasn't until after winning the Burdines Invitational as an amateur in 1969 that Carner finally turned professional. She was also undefeated in Curtis Cup singles (4-0-1). "That first U.S. Amateur victory was a huge thrill," Carner has said. "I really loved playing head-to-head, and I enjoyed all my battles in the Curtis Cup matches."

Realizing there was nothing left to accomplish as an amateur, she turned professional and in just 12 seasons had won 35 events to qualify for the LPGA Hall of Fame. "Some people are afraid to win, others are afraid to lose," Carner has said. "I think winning is a lot more fun."

Carner's second victory as a professional came in the 1971 U.S. Women's Open, making her the only golfer in history to win the U.S. Girls' Junior, the U.S. Women's Amateur and the U.S. Women's Open titles. She won the Women's Open again in 1976 and 42 LPGA titles in a 14-year period from 1970 to 1984. Three times she was Player of the Year, five times the Vare Trophy winner, and all the time, the clubhouse leader in body language, crowd interaction and exhortations.

Win or lose, "Big Momma" was quite a show. "Concentration and getting involved with the shot are important, but if I get too serious I can't play," Carner said. "I relieve the pressure by light chatter with the gallery, although I never get into conversation. I enjoy being able to show more emotion as a professional. I get so enthused with the golf that if the ball is going for the pin or in the cup, I am the first one to yell."

THE CARNER RECORD

Major Championship Victories . . . 2
   U.S. Women's Open: 1971, 1976
Other Significant Victories
   U.S. Girls' Junior: 1956
   Women's Amateur: 1957, 1960, 1962, 1966, 1968
Curtis Cup Teams 4
   (6-3-1) . . 1958, 1960, 1962, 1964
LPGA Rookie of the Year: 1970
LPGA Titles 42
Vare Trophy: 1974, 1975, 1981, 1982, 1983
Leading Money Winner: 1974, 1982, 1983
Player of the Year: 1974, 1981, 1982
Bob Jones Award: 1981

Dr. Cary Middlecoff

Cary Middlecoff is often remembered for his glacial pace of play, his occasionally volcanic temper, and his nickname Doc, which he earned for being a qualified dentist. What he should be remembered as is one of the few players ever to master the game young and then never lose his grip on it.

Middlecoff won his third tournament as a pro, in 1947, and at least one more in every year until his retirement in 1961. When he hung up his spikes, his 37 career victories were seventh on the PGA TOUR's all-time list, and he had also bagged a U.S. Open and two Masters titles.

Middlecoff won the Memphis city championship and Tennessee State Amateur while still a teenager, took one collegiate tournament by 29 strokes while at the University of Mississippi, and later became the first amateur to win the North and South Open, in 1945, while playing in the final group with Ben Hogan and Gene Sarazen.

"I'd give the world to have a swing like that," Bobby Jones once said.

Middlecoff was born in Halls, Tenn., and earned the nickname "The Ghost" as a boy because he was always haunting the town's country clubs, looking for tips on his game. He was a big kid (eventually growing to 6'2") who was more interested in knocking the stuffing out of the ball than perfecting any technique. Later in life he would use his tremendous length off the tee to overpower golf courses and opponents alike.

Middlecoff had nearly given up golf for dentistry when World War II convinced him otherwise. After serving 18 months of active duty, and filling some 7,000 teeth, he decided to give the PGA TOUR a whirl, with the caveat that if he wasn't successful within two years he would go back to drilling teeth instead of 2-irons. At the Charlotte Open in his rookie year, Middlecoff tied the course record in the final round and took home the $2,000 winner's check. He never looked back.

Two years later, he won his first major, the 1949 U.S. Open at Medinah. The most dominant performance of Middlecoff's career came at the 1955 Masters, which he won by a then-record seven strokes, stoked by an 86-foot putt for eagle on the 13th hole during the third round. When he held off Ben Hogan and Julius Boros at the next year's U.S. Open at Oak Hill, Middlecoff established himself as one of the premier golfers of the 1950s.

At the 1957 U.S. Open, Middlecoff shot back-to-back 68s to make up eight strokes and force a playoff with Dick Mayer, but it was memorable for other reasons. Mayer showed up for the playoff with a camping stool, an unsubtle comment on Middlecoff's slow play, which stemmed from an unnatural fastidiousness about his alignment. Indeed, according to the writer Dan Jenkins, Middlecoff's fellow pros used to joke that he had given up dentistry because no patient could hold his mouth open that long. How much Mayer's stunt perturbed Middlecoff is unknown, but he shot a woeful 79 to lose the Open by seven strokes.

Middlecoff was deliberate in other ways. At top of his languid backswing he came to a visible stop. Middlecoff was a pithy commentator on the game who worked for several years as a television analyst. Among his more memorable phrases were, "Nobody wins the Open. It wins you," and "Anyone who hasn't been nervous, or hasn't choked somewhere down the line, is an idiot." Middlecoff's theories on the golf swing, collected in a book appropriately title *The Golf Swing*, are considered among the most understandable ever written. Which is not surprising, considering the game always came so easily to him.

THE MIDDLECOFF RECORD

Major Championship Victories . . . 3
  U.S. Open: 1949, 1956
  Masters: 1955
PGA TOUR Victories 37
Ryder Cup Teams 3
  (2-3-1) 1953, 1955, 1959
Vardon Trophy: 1956

Robert Trent Jones

Robert Trent Jones did not invent golf course architecture, it only seems that way. In a career that has spanned nearly 70 years, Jones has built or rebuilt some 400 courses in 43 states in the U.S. and 34 countries worldwide, with more than three dozen of them having played host to national or international championships. Still, the numbers tell only part of the story.

Jones made an art form of heroic architecture, institutionalizing the risk-reward shot in modern courses. With his oft-quoted philosophy to make every hole a hard par but an easy bogey, he has also had a profound impact on tournament golf. Jones built or remodeled some of the most muscular courses the pros have ever faced, including Firestone, Hazeltine, Spyglass Hill, Baltusrol, and Oak Hill. In his early years Jones's designs often engendered criticism as too severe, and the complaints reached a crescendo when he remodeled Oakland Hills for the 1951 U.S. Open. When a victorious Ben Hogan boasted of having brought that "monster to its knees," and Herbert Warren Wind followed with a laudatory — and widely read — article in *The New Yorker*, Jones was introduced to a mass audience and the cult of the golf course architect was born.

Jones was born in Ince, England, in 1906, and he emigrated with his parents to Rochester, N.Y., three years later. He was a scratch golfer by his early teens but an ulcer sidelined him from tournament competition. A high school dropout, Jones was working as a draftsman for a railroad company when Donald Ross came to Rochester to build Oak Hill. Jones was fascinated with what he saw, and in short order, he parlayed some golf connections into a special entry to Cornell University. There he designed his own course of studies to prepare for a career in golf course architecture, and although his special status precluded a degree, he learned his lessons well enough that in 1930 he formed a partnership with Canadian architect Stanley Thompson.

Jones's first masterwork came in 1948, when he collaborated with Bobby Jones on Peachtree Golf Club in Atlanta (to avoid confusion, Jones adopted the name Trent, from the river in England, and it stuck). Peachtree had all the design features that would become Trent Jones hallmarks: enormous, subtly-contoured greens that offered a host of pin positions, expansive tees that permitted numerous setups, unobtrusive hazards and a fanatical devotion to preserving the land's natural beauty. Among the many architects to be influenced by these design features are Jones's two sons, Robert, Jr., and Rees, both prominent architects in their own right.

Of course, it's impossible to duplicate the real thing, in part because Trent Jones brought an unmistakable showmanship to his craft. This was never more evident than in the wake of his remodeling of Baltusrol's Lower Course, in 1952, when a particularly outspoken member criticized the newly-designed fourth hole, a 194-yard par-3 over water. Eager to rebuff the sniping, Jones grabbed a spoon and heroically marched his critic and a few bystanders to the tee. He took a swing, and the ball took one hop and dove into the hole.

"Gentlemen," said Jones,"I think the hole is eminently fair."

THE JONES RECORD

Trent Jones has designed 216 courses in the United States and 45 overseas. He has also remodeled 126 courses around the world.

22 U.S. Opens and 12 PGA Championships have been played on his courses.

Betsy Rawls

There is not a more respected woman in the game of golf than Betsy Rawls. Her 55 career victories rank behind only Kathy Whitworth, Mickey Wright and Patty Berg, and her four U.S. Women's Opens are only one behind the record established by Babe Didrikson Zaharias. But for all her accomplishments on the course, Rawls was just as admired for her excellence at every level of the game.

The USGA could not have honored a more deserving person than Rawls when it presented her the Bob Jones Award for distinguished service in 1996. "Betsy has always been committed to work and dedicated to the game," said Wright. "I can think of only two women who have achieved as much, not only as players but for their lifetime contributions, and that's Betsy and Patty Berg."

Rawls did not swing a club until she was 17. Four years later, she won the 1949 Texas Amateur, and, in 1950, she finished second behind Babe Zaharias in the Women's Open. After graduating Phi Beta Kappa from the University of Texas, she turned professional in 1951 and made the Open her first victory. She led the LPGA in earnings in 1952, won her second Women's Open in 1953, and her third in 1957. Her biggest year was 1959, when she won 10 times, including the LPGA Championship and the Western Open, and the Vare Trophy. Her biggest thrill was winning the LPGA Championship in 1969, because she had reached a point where she wasn't sure if she could win again.

"I thought I was going to be a winner, and as I went along, winning became easier and easier," Rawls has said. "It was something I expected to do. I always played well under pressure because it didn't bother me,

which is why I won so many tournaments. I don't take much credit for it, but I could perform under tense situations. It was my physical makeup to allow that to happen."

When Rawls joined the Tour, there were about 20 players and 20 tournaments. She served under Zaharias as the LPGA secretary, and headed the tournament committee that set up the courses, gave rulings, made pairings, kept statistics and did the bookkeeping. The rest of the year was spent barnstorming for Wilson Sporting Goods with Patty Berg. They would do upwards of 120 clinics a year, traveling the country in a car.

"No one who turned professional at that time did it to make money, to get endorsements or to be on television," Rawls says. "It was purely for the sake of playing competitive golf and wanting to prove yourself. I thoroughly enjoyed it then, and all of the 25 years that I played. I never got tired of it, never woke up and said, 'I hate having to go to the golf course this morning.' I always looked forward to playing."

When she retired from tournament golf in 1975, Rawls became a tournament director for the LPGA, and later took over as executive director of the McDonald's Championship, which later became the LPGA Championship. She has also served on the USGA's Rules Committee and the LPGA Tournament Sponsors Association. In 1980, she became the first woman to officiate at the men's U.S. Open.

"Anybody who can make a living in golf is lucky," Rawls said. "Then to receive all the benefits accorded to me in the process . . . well, it makes me feel fortunate. It's more than I could possibly deserve."

THE RAWLS RECORD

Major Championship Victories . . . 8
U.S. Women's Open: 1951, 1953, 1957, 1960
Women's Western Open: 1952, 1959
LPGA: 1959, 1969

LPGA Tour Victories 55

Vare Trophy: 1959
Leading Money Winner: 1952, 1959
Bob Jones Award: 1996
Tournament director for the LPGA for six years.
First woman to serve on the Rules Committee for the men's U.S. Open.

Tom Watson

Of all the players who challenged Jack Nicklaus's supremacy, Tom Watson carved out the greatest legacy.

Watson has won 33 events on the PGA TOUR, including two Masters and a U.S. Open, and a remarkable five British Opens.

Beginning in 1977, Watson won six PGA TOUR Player of the Year awards, and he led the money list five times. Yet it was his head-to-head victories against Nicklaus, ten years his senior, that cemented him as a player for the ages.

The first came at the 1977 Masters, where Watson countered Nicklaus's fourth-round charge with four birdies on the closing six holes to win by two. Four months later in the British Open at Turnberry, the two engaged in the most intense and highest caliber sustained battle in the history of major championship golf. Tied after 36 holes, they were paired together in in the final two rounds. Nicklaus shot 65-66, only to be beaten by Watson's 65-65.

Then in 1982, Nicklaus, gunning for a record fifth U.S. Open, held the lead down the stretch at Pebble Beach. Again Watson counterattacked, finally pitching in for a birdie from from deep rough off the 17th hole to produce one of the most dramatic shots ever seen. When he also birdied the 72nd hole, he had won by two strokes and earned his only U.S. Open title.

Watson was born Sept. 4, 1949, in Kansas City, Mo. An all-around athlete growing up, the fresh-faced but fiercely competitive Watson was nicknamed "Huckleberry Dillinger." After a good but not spectacular junior career, Watson attended Stanford, where he graduated with a degree in psychology and showed occasional but not sustained brilliance as a golfer.

But once Watson joined the PGA TOUR, he showed a determination to excel that soon set him apart. "Tom would never tolerate a weakness," said Lanny Wadkins. "He'd go to the practice tee and beat at it until the darn thing went away."

Still, Watson had trouble winning early in his career. At the 1974 U.S. Open at Winged Foot, he took a one-stroke lead into the final round, only to shoot a 79 that dropped him to fifth. He also led after 36 holes the next year at Medinah but again finished weakly. Watson once said, "I learned how to win by losing and not liking it." And he also learned from Byron Nelson, who later became his teacher and mentor.

At the British Open at Carnoustie, Watson holed a 20-footer for birdie on the 72nd hole to get into a playoff with Jack Newton, and prevailed by one stroke in the 18-hole playoff. It would start a pattern of success in the oldest major that best reflected Watson's indefatigable character as a player. Watson would win the claret jug four more times, in 1977, 1980, 1982 and 1983. "Tom takes a deep-rooted pleasure at the prospect of the challenge," said his friend and former USGA president Frank "Sandy" Tatum. "What evolves is the focusing of an unusual intelligence on what he is setting out to do."

Although Watson was a long hitter who had frequent streaks of superb ball striking and birdie runs, he was even better as a scrambler who could manufacture good scores with what became known as "Watson pars." During his reign as the best player in the game, Watson was a fearless putters who frequently ran birdie chances well by the hole, but seemingly never missed the comebacker.

After his glory years ended with his last money title in 1984, Watson's putting declined, and he has won only twice since. He has continued to contend in the PGA, the only major he has never won, and remains one of the finest players from tee to green in the game.

THE WATSON RECORD

Major Championship Victories . . . 8
  Masters: 1977, 1981
  U.S. Open: 1982
  British Open: 1975, 1977, 1980, 1982, 1983

PGA TOUR Victories 33

Ryder Cup Teams 5
  (10-4-1) . 1977, 1981, 1983, 1989
  Captain 1993

Vardon Trophy: 1977, 1978, 1979

Leading Money Winner: 1977, 1978, 1979, 1980, 1984

Peter Thomson

Peter Thomson was the thinking man's golfer. His clean, brisk game was based on cold logic and a gift for reducing things to their simplest essentials. His style was free of the extraneous, so that the path he would take to victory seemed a remarkably straight line.

Between 1954 and 1965, the Australian won the British Open five times. He was the only man other than Young Tom Morris to win it three times consecutively. He won 26 times in Europe, 19 times in Australia and New Zealand and 11 more times in Asia and Japan. He played only a few seasons in America, garnering one victory, the 1956 Texas Open, where he closed with a 63 and defeated Cary Middlecoff and Gene Littler in a playoff.

Thomson was best on fast-running courses where judging the bounce and run of the ball was more important than long hitting. Mostly for that reason, he did not excel when playing on the well-watered and longer courses in the United States. Other than his victory in Texas, Thomson's best showing in a U.S. event was a fourth place in the 1956 U.S. Open and a fifth in the 1957 Masters. He never played in the PGA Championship.

That apparent void in his record is the reason Thomson's victory in the 1965 British Open at Birkdale is considered his finest hour. By that year, most of America's most prominent professionals were competing in the oldest championship, and Thomson beat them all handily.

But even without that victory, Thomson's championship mettle is beyond reproach. With his confident gait and serene smile, he had the self-possessed aura of a winner. "I never saw a golfer who seemed so assured of his destiny," wrote Pat Ward-Thomas. "There is about him the unmistakable air of success."

Thomson was born Aug. 23, 1929, in Melbourne, Australia. As a boy, his first strokes were made on the sly at a nine-hole club named Royal Park. When the members saw his talent, he was given playing privileges, and by age 15 was the club champion.

After a two-year apprenticeship as an assistant pro on courses along Melbourne's famed Sandbelt, Thomson turned professional and quickly dominated Australian golf. "I sensed he had that inevitable something when I first set eyes on him," said the great Australian pro, Norman von Nida. As a young professional, he was profoundly influenced by friendships with Bobby Locke, Ben Hogan and Sam Snead.

Thomson was gifted with a true affinity for being in the thick of the tense closing moments of a championship. "That was the real thrill of it for me," he said in his biography. "I've seen a lot of people find themselves in that situation, and I suspect that very few of them like it, but I really enjoyed it."

By temperament and design, Thomson indeed seemed pressure-proof. His grip was light, his manner at address brisk, and his motion through the ball graceful and devoid of much physical effort. He was a reliable and occasionally brilliant putter. "There were no frills," said von Nida, "so virtually nothing could go wrong."

Above all, Thomson had a head for the game. "The most important facets of golf are careful planning, calm and clear thinking and the ordinary logic of common sense," he once wrote. It was the same cool detachment with which he separated his competitive self from the rest of his life. He was truly a balanced man in a world that usually requires obsessive and narrow dedication. Thomson enjoyed reading, the opera and painting. He ran for elected office in Australia in 1982, narrowly losing. After his competitive rounds, when he was abroad, he often wrote cogent dispatches and columns for the *Melbourne Herald.* Later in is career, he designed golf courses, especially in Asia, where he was also instrumental in establishing professional tours. His diverse interests were a big reason why he chose not to uproot himself for America like other Australian golfers.

Thomson did give the SENIOR TOUR a brief try, and the results were outstanding. In 1985, he won nine tournaments, a record he shares with Hale Irwin.

THE THOMSON RECORD

Major Championship Victories	5
British Open: 1954, 1955,1956, 1958, 1965	
Total Tournaments Won	57
PGA TOUR Victories	1
European Tour Victories	26
Australasia Tour Victories	19
SENIOR PGA TOUR Victories	11

Bob Harlow

Visionary. Trailblazer. Father of the PGA TOUR. This was Bob Harlow, the man who packaged and promoted golf in this country into an entertainment business. What were innovations for Harlow are institutions today, ideas such as a year-round schedule, the concept of a volunteer system and the PGA's Merchandise Show. "He was the one who really put it in some kind of order, setting up the basic framework that exists today," said golf writer Al Barkow. He did this right after the Depression, selling golf not only as a sport, but as a product. He was the game's first mover and shaker.

Harlow's background was newspapers, but he loved the theatre and reading *Variety*, the show business bible. As a youth, he had been a performer, and he married a woman who was a concert singer. His first connection to golf was through the management of Walter Hagen, but that was a no-brainer. Hagen was a showman, and Harlow wrote most of his material. It was a great marriage.

Hagen was the box office, but it took more than a marquee for Harlow to sell the sport in America. Being the son of a minister certainly helped. Sitting through those Sunday services taught Harlow how to proselytize and raise money. He would go into towns and cities and convince the local Chambers of Commerce and the community leaders that playing host to golf tournaments was the way to go. He would get businesses, country clubs, radio stations and newspapers behind the event, and then he would go on to the next town or city, doing the same deal all over.

The PGA of America hired him for $100 a week to do this job, but there were spinoffs that Harlow could cash in on. As the manager for Hagen, Paul Runyan, Horton Smith and Ed Dudley, Harlow practically controlled the show,

so he would book these marathon exhibition swings where his players would play against each other, five to six times a week, for over a month. They would do this traveling through the American heartland, states like Missouri, Illinois, Oklahoma, Texas, Kansas, Nebraska, Colorado, Utah and Idaho.

In November 1930, Harlow proposed the idea of a year-round tournament circuit. He introduced the concept of public relations and published the first media guide called the *Tournament Players Record Book*. In it, he wrote: "Entertaining of newspapermen is recommended."

Harlow was a master of "spin." During the Depression, he announced that there would be "fewer and better tournaments" for the 1934–1935 season. Purses dropped as low as $1,500, but Harlow kept the TOUR afloat. "The Tournament Bureau of the PGA is working for a number of worthwhile purposes," Harlow wrote. "First to keep the game of golf before the sports-loving public so that enthusiasm may be maintained in a game which is getting plenty of competition from other sports. The second is to provide a great deal of competition for our professionals so that they can maintain a high standard of play and that new players may be developed."

The PGA eventually felt that Harlow had too many irons in the fire, and elected to replace him in 1936 with Fred Corcoran. At age 57, he went on to form the weekly magazine *Golf World*. The idea, in the words of golf writer Charles Price, was "put the whole community of golf on a party line." Moving to Pinehurst, N.C., he became publicity director for America's golf capital and publisher, writer and photographer for *Golf World*.

There were never enough jobs for Bob Harlow, and it can be said, he did them all well.

THE HARLOW RECORD

Business Manager, Walter Hagen:
1921-1929

Tournaments Manager, PGA: 1930-1935

Founder, *Golf World* magazine: 1947

Raymond Floyd

Raymond Floyd carried an aura as a competitor and a winner that drew fear from his rivals whenever his name went on a leaderboard, which it did during four different decades.

In notching 22 PGA TOUR victories, including four major championships, from 1963 to 1992, Floyd distinguished himself as a player without a discernible weakness, and whose strengths were a superb short game and an obvious mental toughness. The latter was manfested in his distinctive stare, the look of complete concentration that invariably took over his features when he was in contention for a title. "I've seen Raymond win without it, but I've never seen him lose with it," said his wife, Maria, the person Floyd maintains has been the key figure in his long career.

When Floyd's game was on, he was capable of some of the hottest 72-hole forays ever seen. In 1976, he won the Masters by eight strokes with a then-record-tying score of 271, using a 5-wood to consistently hit the par-5s in two and playing them in 16 under par for the week. At the 1982 PGA Championship at Southern Hills, Floyd was again on fire, opening with a record 63 and going wire-to-wire again to win by three.

Along with his explosiveness, Floyd had longevity. He and Sam Snead are the only players ever to win official events in four different decades. In 1992, he became the first player to win on the PGA TOUR and SENIOR PGA TOUR in the same year.

Floyd was born Sept. 4, 1942, in Fort Bragg, N.C. His father was a golf professional in the military managing a driving range and later a golf course at Fort Bragg. At 17, Floyd won the National Jaycees, but almost became a professional baseball player before turning down an offer to pitch in the Cleveland Indians farm system.

He joined the TOUR in 1963, and won in his 11th start in the St. Petersburg Open. Floyd was obviously talented, a long hitter with a gifted short game, but he only won once more in the next six years. By his own admission, the young Floyd was as interested in having a good time away from the golf course than getting the most from his game on it.

But in 1969, he set a goal to win $100,000, win a major championship and make the Ryder Cup team. He did all three, while taking the 1969 PGA Championship. Still, Floyd did not become a truly dedicated player until his marriage to Maria Fraietta in 1973. "She got me to respect my ability," said Floyd. "I decided to find out how good I could be, and it made a huge difference." Beginning in 1975, Floyd averaged a victory a year for the next 17 years. In 1983, he won the Vardon Trophy.

Floyd's crowning achievement was winning the 1986 U.S. Open at Shinnecock Hills G.C. Floyd had never played particularly well at the Open, posting only two top-10 finishes in his previous 18 tries. But the spacious feel of Shinnecock brought out his best. He played controlled golf, put together a flawless back nine on Sunday, and won by two strokes.

The only major Floyd never won was the British Open, where he tied for second at St. Andrews in 1978 and was joint third in 1981.

Floyd was one of the first players to combine tremendous power with a soft touch, making him an important player in the evolution of the modern game. Floyd's short game is considered exemplary, and he is often acknowledged as one of the greatest chippers the game has ever seen.

THE FLOYD RECORD

Major Championship Victories . . .	4
Masters: 1976	
U.S. Open: 1986	
PGA: 1969, 1982	
PGA TOUR Victories	22
SENIOR PGA TOUR Victories . .	13
Ryder Cup Teams	9
(12-16-2) . . 1969, 1975, 1977, 1981, 1983, 1985, 1991, 1993	
Captain.	1989
Vardon Trophy: 1983	

Nancy Lopez

The year was 1978, and the Ladies Professional Golf Association was suffering an identity crisis. From Roswell, N.M., came an unidentified flying star, a Mexican-American girl whose father owned an auto-body shop. She won the state amateur when she was 12, two U.S. Girls' Junior titles, an NCAA title, and, in 1975, she finished second in the U.S. Women's Open. If this wasn't the savior, then God knows who was.

Her name was Nancy Lopez, and it wasn't long before everybody just called her Nancy. She won five consecutive tournaments in 1978, and everybody sort of hitched a ride on her skirt tails: the press, the fans, the sponsors, even the rest of the women playing the sport. These were magical times for women's golf, and nobody seemed to want to get in her way.

She won nine times that year, including the LPGA Championship, eight times in 1979 and she was the nicest person in the world. "After my first year I thought, 'I could be a flash in the pan,' and I was also determined to prove I was not," Lopez has said. "I was determined not to fall on my face, though it is easy enough to choke yourself to death trying to win."

Looking back on these years, Jaime Diaz wrote in *Sports Illustrated* that Lopez had burst on the scene with as much charisma as anyone since Babe Didrikson Zaharias.

Not even Zaharias had become a legend so fast. She was all of 21 years old, and the veterans marveled not only at her golfing ability, but her poise and maturity.

"Never in my life have I seen such control from someone so young," said Mickey Wright.

"They've got the wrong person playing Wonder Woman," said Judy Rankin.

"We're all trying to steal Nancy's birth-control pills, but so far we've been unsuccessful," said JoAnne Carner.

After marrying baseball star Ray Knight, she struggled balancing her career with motherhood. By the time she was 30, Nancy Lopez still had won enough tournaments (35) to qualify for the LPGA Hall of Fame. At that point, she was Player of the Year three times, Vare Trophy winner three times, and her stroke average in 1985 of 70.73 was an LPGA record.

Lopez had the ability to close. She was the youngest qualifier for the LPGA Hall of Fame, and had to wait six months to be inducted as the rules for admission required that a player be on tour for 10 years. "I feel honored to be with the other women in the Hall of Fame," Lopez said. "I have always respected them and what they have done for women's golf. I look at each player, and some are already legends while others will become legends as time goes by. I feel I'm a great now, being in the Hall of Fame, having accomplished what I've done and being with the greatest golfers. I feel great that I can say I'm one of them."

With her sights set on 50 victories, it would be fitting that Lopez reached the milestone someday at the U.S. Women's Open. She won her 48th tournament in 1997, and at the age of 40, finished second for the fourth time in the Open. She shot four rounds in the 60s — the first woman to do so — but lost by a stroke to Alison Nicholas.

"I'd love to win the Open," Lopez once said. "But I've had enough good things in life that I won't be shattered if I don't."

THE LOPEZ RECORD

Major Championship Victories . . . 3
  LPGA: 1978, 1985, 1989
LPGA Tour Victories 48
Curtis Cup Teams 1
  (2-0-0) 1976
Vare Trophy: 1978, 1979, 1985
Leading Money Winner: 1978, 1979, 1985
Bob Jones Award: 1998

Roberto De Vicenzo

The world will always remember Roberto De Vicenzo for what he lost, not for what he won — for that careless mistake he made at the 1968 Masters, signing an incorrect scorecard that had him making a par and not a birdie on the 17th hole that Sunday afternoon — and thus, his uttering of the immortal golf quote, "What a stupid I am."

Yet, there is so much more to De Vicenzo's career and the contributions he made to golf around the world, that what occurred in the scorer's tent at Augusta National should not overshadow the man's legacy. Roberto de Vicenzo won over 230 golf tournaments, including the 1967 British Open at Hoylake, where he held off the Sunday charges of Jack Nicklaus and Gary Player to become, at 44, the oldest winner of the world's oldest golf championship.

Facing success and catastrophe and treating those twin imposters the same inspired British golf writer Peter Dobereiner to use the Rudyard Kipling quote when giving De Vicenzo his due. In Dobereiner's words, "By that standard, De Vicenzo is a giant of a man because he faced the greatest triumph and the most devastating disaster which the game of golf can provide." The United States Golf Association and the Golf Writers Association of America agreed, presenting De Vicenzo with the Bob Jones and William Richardson Awards, respectively, in 1970.

All the trophies he captured didn't mean as much to De Vicenzo as the friends he made traveling the globe. He won national opens in Belgium, Brazil, Chile, Colombia, Holland, France, Germany, Jamaica, Mexico, Panama, Peru, Spain, Uruguay and Argentina, a country he represented 17 times in the World Cup. Essayist Jack Whitaker once said that if golf were war, Roberto would have conquered more countries than Alexander the Great. But golf was not war to De Vicenzo. And that is what made him so loved.

Born in Buenos Aires on April 14, 1923, De Vicenzo learned the game as a caddy's assistant. He turned professional at age 15 and won his first of nine Argentine Open titles six years later. Three-time British Open Champion Henry Cotton once said there were very few professionals in the business who would not take the play through the green of the Argentine golfing master Roberto De Vicenzo, and his game never left him. At 51 he won the PGA Seniors Championship and in 1980, at the age of 57, the inaugural U.S. Senior Open.

He believed in hard practice, routinely hitting 400 balls a day and maintaining a slow pace. "If you hurry," he would say, "then nothing seems to go right." He'd visualize a shot, pick a club and hit. His method was simple to watch, and it would hold up under pressure.

It did that final round at the Masters in 1969. What's lost behind that staggering mistake made by fellow competitor Tommy Aaron and signed for by De Vicenzo is that Roberto shot what has been called one of the greatest rounds in major championship history. He took only 65 strokes around Augusta National that day, including a bogey at the 18th, on his 45th birthday. His 31 on the front side started with an eagle 2 at the first and tied the course record. It should have been good enough to tie Bob Goalby and set up a playoff which, had he won, would have given Roberto De Vicenzo both the British Open and Masters titles at the same time.

THE DE VICENZO RECORD

Total Worldwide Victories 230

Major Championship Victories . . . 1
British Open: 1967

PGA TOUR Victories 4

Other Significant Victories
PGA Seniors: 1974
U.S. Senior Open: 1980

SENIOR PGA TOUR Victories . . . 3

Represented Argentina in World Cup 17 times

Bob Jones Award: 1970

William Richardson Award: 1970

Jim Barnes

Known as "Long Jim" because of his 6'4" height, lanky build and long hitting, Barnes won four major championships in an era best known for the exploits of Walter Hagen and Gene Sarazen.

The tallest of the champions of the first half of the century, Barnes won the first PGA Championship ever played, in 1916, and won the next one, played in 1919. He won the 1921 U.S. Open at the Columbia C.C. by nine strokes, the largest margin of victory in this century, the 1925 British Open at Prestwick, when he came from five strokes behind after Macdonald Smith faltered with a final round 82. He is one of only eight golfers to have won those three. He also won the Western Open three times, which in his day, was considered an elite championship. He never played in the Masters, which began in 1934. On the U.S. TOUR, he is credited with 20 career victories and 14 seconds.

In his U.S. Open victory, Barnes opened with a 69 to take a three-stroke lead and was never challenged. When Barnes won, he was given the trophy by President Warren Harding, making him the only player in history to receive the U.S. Open trophy from the President of the United States.

Barnes was runner-up in the PGA to Walter Hagen in 1921 and 1924. He was also second in the 1922 British Open. He won the North and South Open in 1916, his first victory, and again in 1919. In 1916, he also won a PGA Stroke Play Championship played after the match-play event, but it was never counted as official.

His last victory came at the 1937 Long Island Open, when he was 50 years old.

Gene Sarazen, who feuded with Barnes because of what he considered the older man's brusque manner, nevertheless rated him the finest 5-iron player he had ever seen. In 1940, Barnes was made one of the 12 original inductees into the PGA Hall of Fame.

Barnes was born in Leland, England, in 1887. At age 15, he was made an assistant pro. He emigrated to San Francisco in 1906, but never became an American citizen, remaining an intensely patriotic Cornishman. Still, he remained attached to his native country, playing in the British Open regularly and finishing in the top eight seven times between 1920 and 1928.

In 1919, Barnes produced the book *Picture Analysis of Golf Strokes*, which became one of the most widely read instructionals of the day. It featured full photographs of Barnes's strong, compact swing at key points. The book revolutionized printed golf instruction.

"His finish was a model for a tall man who is inclined to spring up too soon after the ball is hit," wrote Bernard Darwin. "Everything he did was pleasant to watch."

Barnes had an angular, serious face that was topped by a thatch of unruly hair that gave him "an aspect which, to the stranger, suggested the Wild West," according to Darwin. He was an intense, quiet competitor who often kept a sprig of clover or grass clamped tightly between his teeth. All his career, he was one of the few players who wore trousers instead of knickers, an "old school" conceit.

Barnes was a man of few words, but he possessed important wisdom, which he imparted when he felt the subject was worthy. He once told the young Jones, "Bobby, you can't always be playing well when it counts. You'll never win golf tournaments until you learn how to score well when you're playing badly." The statement made a profound impact on Jones, who later wrote. "This is perhaps what I learned to do best of all."

Barnes died in 1966.

THE BARNES RECORD

Major Championship Victories . . . 4
  U.S. Open: 1921
  British Open: 1925
  PGA: 1916, 1919
Other Significant Victories
  North and South Open: 1916, 1919
  Western Open: 1914, 1917, 1919
PGA TOUR Victories 20

William C. Campbell

The era is sadly over when some of America's best golfers played the game as amateurs, and it was often what these men and women stood for, that was as important as the trophies they won. Born in West Virginia, educated at Princeton, Bill Campbell never had the desire to chase the buck. After college, and the service, he stayed at home, opened an insurance business, served in the legislature, and played golf because he loved playing golf. He played it at the highest level, and became one of the game's most distinguished statesmen.

Only Chick Evans (49) played in the U.S. Amateur more times than Campbell (37) — and not even Evans played in 33 consecutively, as Campbell did from 1941-1977. That he finally won it in 1964, at the age of 41, is a testimony to the doggedness of his pursuit. He won it just after Jack Nicklaus and Deane Beman turned pro, and just before names like Bob Murphy, Bruce Fleisher, Steve Melnyk, Lanny Wadkins, Craig Stadler and Jerry Pate came along to snatch the title in the midst of their college careers. The next day, he was back in his office.

"We hadn't reached the point yet where the better amateurs would routinely turn pro," Campbell said. "We weren't into the college golf syndrome where it was a scholarship leading to the TOUR. It was just the beginning of that. We had quite a number of people like myself who were fair players, who wanted to play competitive golf but had no intention of being professional golfers. The amateur game was pretty lively

without being dominated by college golf. It was a fun thing. You'd run into the same people year after year. You grew older as they did. Over that period of the late '40s to the late '60s, I had the pleasure of being a part of that."

It once was written in *Golf Journal* that Bill Campbell was a professional at being an amateur golfer, and that sums it up. He is a man who will go to extremes in order not to take advantage of an opponent, but the gentleman golfer is also the personification of determination. In the 1947 U.S. Amateur at Pebble Beach, he hit his first two drives out of bounds, but chipped in to halve the hole and went on to win the match.

Campbell won 15 West Virginia State Amateur titles, three West Virginia State Opens, the North and South Amateur four times and was undefeated in Walker Cup singles competition, holding a 7-0-1 record in the eight matches he played between 1951 and 1975. That also gives Campbell a unique record: Most Years Between U.S. Walker Cup Selections (24).

Campbell also served as U.S. Golf Association president from 1982-1983, and was the third American nominated to be captain of the Royal and Ancient Golf Club of St. Andrews, Scotland. When he accepted the position, Campbell wanted to reaffirm the manners that go with golf and remind everyone that it is a game of relationships and of dignity and of self-respect.

"It is an honorable game, an honorable institution, if you will, so that people shouldn't need policemen to keep them straight," Campbell said. "That goes with being a golfer."

THE CAMPBELL RECORD

Major Championship Victories 1
U.S. Amateur: 1964
(Played in 37 Amateurs, including a record 33 straight from 1941 to 1977.)

Walker Cup Teams 8
(11-4-3) . . 1951, 1953, 1955, 1957, 1965, 1967, 1971, 1975
Captain. 1955

Other Significant Victories
North and South Amateur: 1950, 1953, 1957, 1961
West Virginia State Amateur: 15 times
Mexican Amateur: 1956
U.S. Senior Amateur: 1979, 1980
Bob Jones Award: 1956
President, USGA: 1982, 1983

Paul Runyan

No player in the history of golf was a more feared little man than Paul Runyan. His career was the fulfillment of his goal to be the best truly light-hitting player who ever lived.

Slight at 5-7, 125 pounds, Runyan could produce little power with a swing that featured a pronounced sway — in tournaments where his drives were measured, he barely averaged 230 yards off the tee. But Runyan was deadly straight, a tremendously accurate fairway-wood player, and reliable with the irons. Around and on the greens he was an absolute genius. Throw in killer instinct and Depression-bred toughness and you get the golfer known as "Little Poison."

"Don't let the bad shots get to you," said Runyon. "Don't let yourself become angry. The true scramblers are thick-skinned. And they always beat the whiners."

Between 1930 and 1941, Runyan won 28 times on the PGA TOUR. In 1933, he racked up nine victories, and, in 1934, he won six more and captured the money title the first year such records were kept with a total of $6,767.

He also won the 1934 PGA, beating Craig Wood on the 38th hole. Four years later at Shawnee-on-Delaware, Pa., he won the PGA again, defeating Sam Snead in the final, 8 and 7, in what has become golf history's definitive David vs. Goliath story. Although Snead was outdriving him by 45 yards and more, Runyan kept hitting his fairway wood approaches inside of the stronger man. On the par 5s, where Snead figured to have a decided advantage, Runyan zeroed in from inside 100 yards to birdie six of the seven that were played. "This isn't golf, it's magic," said Snead at one point during the match. Later he would write, "I don't suppose anyone ever got more out their golf game than Paul Runyan. He could get the ball up and down from a manhole."

During that 1938 PGA, Runyan was 24 under par for the 196 holes he played, including 64 con-secutive holes without going over par. He felt he was at his best in match play, in large part because his style of play wore down opponents psychologically, and because of his own nature. "You are in for the fight of your life," he said. "It is just instinctive that I fight."

Paul Runyan was born July 12, 1908, in Hot Springs, Ark. His father was a dairy farmer who assigned his son plenty of chores, but the young Runyan soon gravitated to the town golf club across the road, where he discovered he could make more money caddying and working for the pro. He also became consumed with the new game.

"I had to work for it," he said. "I was not a natural. All the kids in the caddy pen beat me, until I just dug it out and became better."

Runyan was made an apprentice at the club, and would play four holes on the way to school and five on the way back. He recognized early that he would have to have a good short game to be competitive, and he made it his specialty. Byron Nelson chose Runyan as the finest chipper he ever saw, and his wrist-free stroke is a staple of short game method that Runyan later imparted to Gene Littler and Phil Rodgers.

"Through necessity, I began my lifelong devotion to the short game," he wrote, "the searching for shortcuts that would somehow let me compete, and hopefully excel, in a world of stronger players." Runyan ultimately came to regard his short game as an offensive weapon for defeating the course and demoralizing an opponent.

THE RUNYAN RECORD

Major Championship Victories . . . 2
  PGA: 1934, 1938
Other Significant Victories
  PGA Senior: 1961, 1962
PGA TOUR Victories 28
Ryder Cup Teams 2
  (2-2-0) 1933, 1935
Leading Money Winner: 1934

Runyan was tenacious, cocky and indomitable. As late as 1951, he led the U.S. Open at Oakland Hills after three rounds before finishing tied for sixth. He won the PGA Seniors in 1961 and 1962.

"I've taken some pleasure out of being the little guy who has beaten the big fellows," he said. "I would like to be remembered as the best of the truly light hitters." He is.

Gene Littler

Great swings last, and if longevity were the only measure, Gene Littler would have to be considered among the giants of the game. As it was, he won 29 PGA TOUR tournaments including a U.S. Open, was a stalwart in the Ryder Cup across two decades and was a dominant force in the early years of the SENIOR TOUR. But unquestionably, Littler's sustained excellence is what made his career so noteworthy. Only once during the quarter century from 1954 to 1979 did he finish out of the top 60 on the money list, and that was in 1972, when he was sidelined by surgery to remove a cancerous lymph node. Littler bounced back from that to win three tournaments and finish fifth on the money list in 1975 at the age of 45 and two years later he won again, at 47.

Imagine how good Littler's career could have been if he was more passionate about golf. He was often criticized for wanting to spend more time at home in sunny Rancho Santa Fe, Calif., among his vintage car collection than grinding it out on the golf circuit. What allowed Littler to coast was one of the finest natural swings the game has ever known. Gene Sarazen called it "a perfect swing like Sam Snead's - only better," and also talked of Littler's "remarkable physical equipment. He has a pair of wrists like wagon tongues and hands like hams." Littler himself had little explanation for the beauty and simplicity of his swing. "I just put the ball down and hit," he once said. Economy, soft-spokeness and dry wit were part of his makeup. He once said, "I drew a big gallery today. I was paired with Palmer." Former tennis champion Ted Schroeder, father of golfer John Schroeder, summed up his friend thusly: "He gave me a typical Littler conversation. Three yeps, two nopes and two nods."

Littler was born in San Diego in 1930 and first attracted national notice 23 years later, when he sunk an 18-foot birdie putt on the 18th green at the Oklahoma C.C. to win the U.S. Amateur, 1 up, over Dale Morey. Four months later, Littler won the San Diego Open as an amateur, and two days after that, he turned pro. The following year he won four times, earning the nickname "Gene the Machine" for his remarkably consistent ball-striking. Often overlooked was his outstanding short game.

Littler's tendency to fiddle with his near perfect swing led to a pronounced slump (by his lofty standards) in 1957 and 1958, but after changing his grip on the advice of Paul Runyan, he quickly found his old form. In 1961, he won his only professional major, the U.S. Open at Oakland Hills. He closed with a 68 to hold off Bob Goalby and Doug Sanders by one stroke. He came close in two other majors. The closest he came was the 1970 Masters, when he shot a steady 69-70-70-70 to tie Billy Casper, but was outgunned 74 to 69 by his boyhood friend and rival in the playoff that followed. In the 1977 PGA Championship at Pebble Beach, Littler led from the first round, but closed with a 76 and was tied by Lanny Watkins, who won on the third extra hole in the first major championship ever decided in sudden death. Littler also played on seven U.S. Ryder Cup teams, compiling superb 14-5-8 record.

In 1980, Littler became eligible for the SENIOR TOUR and proceeded to win three of his first five tournaments and, in 1981, the Vintage International by a whopping nine strokes. Littler's play surprised no one, because after 30 years "Gene the Machine" winning golf tournaments had come to be expected.

THE LITTLER RECORD

Major Championship Victories . . . 2
  U.S. Amateur: 1953
  U.S. Open: 1961
PGA TOUR Victories 29
SENIOR PGA TOUR Victories . . . 8
Other Senior Victories 9
Walker Cup Teams 1
  (2-0-0) 1953
Ryder Cup Teams 7
  (14-5-8) . . . 1961, 1963, 1965,
    1967, 1969, 1971, 1975
Bob Jones Award: 1973
Ben Hogan Award: 1973

Horton Smith

Horton Smith was one of golf's first boy wonders. In 1929, at the age of 21, he played a PGA TOUR then in its infancy, and won eight of 22 events as well as finishing second six times.

Smith and Paul Runyan were the TOUR's top players during the Depression years. In all, Smith won 30 events and finished second 37 times. A tall, stylish man, he was a smooth swinger with a superb putting touch. Byron Nelson rated Smith the finest putter and chipper of his era, and long after he won his final tournament in 1941, Smith was much sought after by other players for putting advice.

Although Smith was never again quite as good as he had been in 1929, his greatest fame will always come from being the first winner of the Masters, then known as the Augusta National Invitational. In the fourth round, Craig Wood posted 285 early, so Smith knew he needed a 72 or better. After making a 20-foot birdie putt on the 17th hole, he knocked in a four-foot downhiller on the final green to win.

Smith won the event again in 1936. Two strokes behind Harry Cooper with five holes to go, he holed a 45-foot chip on the 68th, an eight-footer on the 69th and a 16-footer on the 71st drenched by torrential rain. That year he also led the TOUR's money list with $7,662.

Smith was born in Springfield, Mo., on May 22, 1908, and took up golf when he was 12. He grew to 6-1½ and 163 pounds, and honed his game as an assistant pro at the Springfield C.C. When he joined the TOUR, he earned the nickname the Missouri Rover by tirelessly travelling the country by car, train and even boat to get to tournaments. Indeed,

one year Smith suffered a fractured wrist when he hit it against a metal sign while stretching his arm out of a car driven by Joe Kirkwood.

Smith is believed to be the first professional to use a sand wedge in competition, a 23-ounce model invented by Texas cotton farmer Edward Kerr McClain. Smith used it in 1930 before it was banned for having a concave face. Smith also gave one to Bobby Jones, who used it to make a crucial birdie in the final round of the British Open at Hoylake on his way to the Grand Slam. Earlier in the year, Smith had won the Savannah Open to become the last man to defeat Jones in competition before his retirement.

According to Herbert Warren Wind, Smith was a student of the game who could be "overlogical, studious, finicky," and probably experimented with his swing too much. Fairly early in his career, Smith's swing lost its compact groove but soon became "the simplified and correct thing it had been."

Smith didn't smoke or drink. He was one of the rare professionals of his day who had attended college, the State Teacher's College in Springfield. Later, showing organizational and public relations talent, Smith would become chairman of the the TOUR's competition committee, and eventually president of the PGA from 1952 to 1954.

Smith was chosen for five Ryder Cup teams, and was never beaten. During his run of victories in 1929, he shot an all-time TOUR low 72-hole score of 245 at the par-64, 4,700-yard Catalina C.C. in California in 1928. He had scores of 63, 58, 61 and 63. He finished third at the U.S. Open in 1930 and 1940, and in the 1930 British Open. He died in 1963.

THE SMITH RECORD

Major Championship Victories . . . 2
  Masters: 1934, 1936
PGA TOUR Victories 30
Other Significant Victories
  French Open: 1928
  Florida Open: 1929
  North and South Open: 1929, 1937
Ryder Cup Teams 5
  (3-0-1) 1929, 1931, 1933, 1935, 1937
Leading Money Winner: 1929
President, PGA: 1952, 1953, 1954

Richard S. Tufts

He has been called The Man Who Was Pinehurst. He served as President of the United States Golf Association, Walker Cup captain and was such a staunch believer in amateurism that he wrote a creed on the subject. This was Richard Tufts, a man who was known in this country quite simply as "Mr. Golf."

While Pinehurst will remain his legacy, it was amateur golf that drove Tufts to be so passionate about the game. "In my mind an amateur is one who competes in a sport for the joy of playing, for the companionship it affords, for health-giving exercise, and for relaxation for more serious matters," were the words Tufts wanted left behind. "As part of his light-hearted approach to the game, he accepts cheerfully all adverse breaks, is considerate of his opponent, plays the game fairly and squarely in accordance with the rules, maintains self-control, and strives to do his best, not in order to win, but rather as a test of his own skill and ability. These are his only interests, and, in them, material considerations have no part. The returns which amateur sport will bring to those who play it in this spirit are greater than those any money can possibly buy."

Tufts was the grandson of James Walker Tufts, the founder of Pinehurst. He grew up in Massachusetts and was described as a man with a strong Yankee conscience and high personal standards. In 1917, after graduating from Harvard, Tufts went off to serve in World War 1. After his tour of duty, he returned to Pinehurst, where his father, Leonard, had been running the resort. Eventually, Richard took over, and brought Pinehurst to new heights. He was the leader of an effort that brought the PGA Championship (1936) and Ryder Cup (1951) to Pinehurst, and he ruled over the resort until relatives sold their stock to Diamondhead

Corp., and the Tufts family lost controlling interest.

Tufts was many things. He served diligently on every USGA committee imaginable, and was part of the delegation, led by Joe Dey, that met in St. Andrews to arrive on a universal code of rules. As time went on, he ascended through the USGA's chain of command, serving as secretary from 1950-1951, vice-president from 1952-1955 and president for two years beginning in 1956.

One of Tufts's legacies was establishing the World Amateur Golf Council and the World Amateur Team Championship. President Dwight D. Eisenhower met with Tufts and delegates of the Council in the Rose Garden of the White House and consented to the naming of the championship prize as the Eisenhower Trophy. The first matches were held at St. Andrews in 1958, with Bob Jones serving as the United States captain.

Tufts was also a protege of Donald Ross, and he built 40 new holes at Pinehurst and revised many more. Ross was the head professional at Pinehurst in 1900, moving South after coming to America from Scotland, where he was given a job at Oakley Country Club in Massachusetts. "There was never anything vulgar about his work," Tufts said of Ross.

Tufts also liked to write, and authored *The Scottish Invasion, An Eightsome of Golfing Badgers*, and perhaps his best book, *The Principles Behind the Rules of Golf.* "If there is one principle more basic than any of the rest, it must be that you play the course as you find it."

Later, he added: "The second great principle of golf is that you put your own ball in play at the start of the hole and play only your own ball and do not touch it before you lift it from the hole."

To Richard Tufts, this was golf the way golf was meant to be played.

THE TUFTS RECORD

USGA President: 1956-1957

Walker Cup Captain: 1963

Bob Jones Award: 1967

Richardson Award: 1950

Harry Cooper

Harry Cooper was one of the finest players and most consistent winners in professional golf in the 1920s and 1930s with but a single void in his career: a major championship title — despite several narrow misses.

Cooper won 30 times on the PGA TOUR between 1925 and 1941, including the Canadian Open and the Los Angeles Open twice each. In 1937, he won seven times, led the money list and won the inaugural Vardon Trophy.

Cooper spent his career around the lead, and he racked up 37 runner-up finishes and 25 thirds in his career. His most disappointing seconds were at the 1927 and 1936 U.S. Opens and at the 1936 Masters, where he was nipped at the end by the hot putting of Horton Smith. He was also second at Augusta in 1938. He reached the semi-finals of the PGA once, losing to Walter Hagen in 1925. He never played in the British Open.

Cooper was born August 4, 1904, in Leatherhead, England, and came to America at age 10. His father, Sid, who had served an apprenticeship under Old Tom Morris at St. Andrews, was the golf professional at Cedar Crest in Dallas. His mother, Alice, also was a fine player who worked in the golf shop and gave lessons.

The young Cooper was a phenom. He won the 1923 Texas PGA at age 18, and repeated the next year. He took his first important title at the 1926 Los Angeles Open. It was there that Damon Runyon dubbed him "Lighthorse" for the speed with which he played and the nimble way he carried himself. At the Los Angeles C.C., he and George Von Elm played the last round in 2 hours and 30 minutes.

While Cooper floated, his caddy labored with a bag filled with 26 clubs.

Cooper was considered a wonderful swinger of the club. When he was young, he had a long, flowing swing, which he describes as "about two inches shorter than John Daly's." Shortly after his victory at Los Angeles, he decided he had to make it more compact, and competed sparingly for about 18 months. When he came back, he had lost some distance, but gained accuracy. It gave birth to another nickname — "Pipeline."

Cooper twice came excruciatingly close to winning the U.S. Open. In 1927 at Oakmont, he led after the third round, but made three 6s on the final 18, and three-putted the 71st hole from eight feet. Then Tommy Armour holed a 10-footer for birdie on the difficult 18th to tie. In the playoff, Cooper led by two after 11, but he double-bogeyed the 16th and lost the playoff, 76-79. In the 1936 Open at Baltusrol, Cooper led by two through three rounds, and finished with a 73 for a record total of 284. While Cooper was being congratulated for his apparent victory, Tony Manero came in with a final-round 67 for 282.

At Augusta in 1936, Cooper led by three after three rounds. However, he got the worst of the wind and rain and finished with a 76. Horton Smith was still two strokes behind with five to play, but birdied two of them while Cooper bogied the 71st.

Nevertheless, in the era of 1930 to 1945, Cooper was ranked by PGA TOUR statistics the fourth-best player behind Byron Nelson, Sam Snead and Horton Smith. "First you've got to be good," Cooper once said, "but then you've got to be lucky."

THE COOPER RECORD

PGA TOUR Victories 30

Vardon Trophy: 1937

Leading Money Winner: 1937

USGA

Patty Sheehan

It is a tribute of a person's fortitude that she is at her best when life seems at its worst. That, then, says it all about Patty Sheehan, who has twice answered adversity with achievement, and who has proven that heart and courage mean as much in golf as talent. When you grow up as a downhill skier, you learn how to pick yourself up, and that's what Sheehan has done.

In 1989, Sheehan lost her house, her trophies, and nearly all of her life savings, in the San Francisco earthquake. She came back the next year to win five tournaments and over $732,000. Nearly all of that money went to pay bills, but it was the tournament she lost in 1990 that represented as much potential devastation to her career as the earthquake did to her financial security.

The U.S. Women's Open was played at the Atlanta Athletic Club. Sheehan had an 11-stroke lead in the third round, and ended up losing it all to Betsy King. As Sheehan later said, "I had owned the Open. It was in my hands. I could break a leg and still shoot well enough to win, but I hadn't been able to do it."

Two years later, Sheehan came to Oakmont C.C. following two consecutive victories. She birdied the 71st and 72nd holes, then went on to defeat Juli Inkster in a playoff. She won the Open again in 1994, but the victory in 1992 at Oakmont was her crowning achievement. "It was such a great comeback from 1990, and emotionally it healed so many wounds," Sheehan told writer Liz Kahn. "It was the most significant win of my career, because I overcame so much doubt. It would have been very hard to live the rest of my life without winning an Open. Now, I feel I'm on vacation from adversity and that 1992 Open victory made me a different person — much happier and more

content. If I never win another tournament, I'm still complete because that was the one I wanted."

Sheehan grew up in Middlebury, Vt., and Lake Tahoe, Nev. Her father, Bobo, was a college ski coach in Vermont and also an Olympic ski coach. As the only girl in the family, Sheehan learned how to compete to survive. She was as good a football player as her three brothers, and at 13, Sheehan was ranked the No. 1 downhill skier for her age in the country. Golf was a secondary sport until Sheehan reached the age of 18, when her handicap was down to scratch and the University of Nevada-Reno offered her a scholarship.

As an amateur, Sheehan won state titles in Nevada and California, the AIAW National Championship for San Jose State, and was runner-up in the 1979 U.S. Women's Amateur Championship. She was undefeated on the 1980 Curtis Cup team, and earned Rookie of the Year honors on the LPGA Tour in 1981.

"I was always very competitive," Sheehan said. "I saw myself as a winner from a very young age. I played with boys all my life, and I seemed to be their equal, if not better. I never thought of myself as anything less than a winner. To be successful, you need drive, determination and a belief in yourself, and some kind of peacefulness about what you're doing."

That attitude resulted in one of the most successful careers in LPGA history. Through the 1997 season, she had won 35 tournaments, including the two Opens, three LPGA Championships and a Dinah Shore. In 1995, she qualified for the Hall of Fame with a win at the SAFECO Classic. "I feel inside I should be there because I stepped up and achieved that level, and there's a place for me beside those greats," Sheehan said. "I'm not bragging. I just feel that way."

THE SHEEHAN RECORD

Major Championship Victories . . . 6
  U.S. Women's Open: 1992, 1994
  LPGA: 1983, 1984, 1993
  Nabisco Dinah Shore: 1996

LPGA Tour Victories 35

LPGA Rookie of the Year: 1981

Vare Trophy: 1984

Dinah Shore

Dinah Shore didn't take up the game until the ripe age of 52, and by her own admission she was not a quick study. "Whenever I break 100 they send up a flare!" she once said. And yet Shore was an illuminating presence for women's golf. Since 1972, her eponymous tournament has been one of the LPGA's most visible. Shore's name helped insure network television coverage back when it was a precious commodity, which in turn helped her tournament set the curve for purse increases. Shore had such a lasting effect on the LPGA Tour that in 1994 she was posthumously made the only honorary member of its prestigious Hall of Fame. "This is not an honor given, it's an honor earned," then LPGA Commissioner Charles Mechem said.

Born Francis Rose Shore in Winchester, Tenn. in 1921 (the Dinah came from a New York disc jockey who forgot her name but remembered she sang a song titled "Dinah), she began her singing career in Memphis. She gained fame on radio in the late 1930s in duets with Frank Sinatra and later on Eddie Cantor's show. She was one of America's first television stars, first on "The Chevy Show," which ran from 1951 to 1961, and later on the Dinah Shore Show, "Dinah's Place," and "Dinah!" She won ten Emmy Awards, nine gold records and a Peabody Award.

Shore took a circuitous route to becoming one of the game's matriarchs. She was stricken with polio when she was 18 months old, and in the years that followed she used sports to bury the disease's legacy. "I began to think that it was some dim, dark secret and that if anybody ever found out they would refuse to play with me because I was different," she said. In junior high, Shore played softball, basketball and ran track, and at Vanderbilt University she made the varsity swimming and fencing teams (and, naturally, was part of the drama club, glee club and cheerleading squad). That she didn't play golf was something of an upset because Shore once described her mother as "one of the finest, most enthusiastic golfers in the state of Tennessee. She died when I was young but her encouragement stayed with me."

Once Shore fell for the game, she fell hard. She became the first female member at Los Angeles's tony Hillcrest Country Club, and her home away from home was Mission Hills in Rancho Mirage, where she had a house off the ninth green. She became the first woman to play in PGA TOUR pro-ams at San Diego and Westchester. Her ambition in golf was to shoot 85, after which, she said, "I will smile forever."

Shore brought to the women's Tour a star quality that was sorely missing. She invited many of the players to appear on her television variety show, and even hooked some up with commercial endorsements. "The Tour was still podunk when we went to Palm Springs, and suddenly we were celebrities," said Jane Blalock, the champion of the inaugural Dinah Shore. "It changed the perception of women's golf." So too did the champion's dive into the lake on Mission Hills's 18th, a frolicking tradition Shore and Amy Alcott started.

For all the good times her tournament generated, Shore's legacy is steeped in far more important matters. "I don't like discrimination on the basis of sex," the First Lady of Golf once said. "Ability is the only thing that matters. The tournament we play is awfully powerful proof of that."

THE SHORE RECORD

Started Dinah Shore Tournament: 1972

Betsy King

It took Betsy King more than seven seasons to win on the LPGA Tour, but her breakthrough led to one of the most phenomenal careers in women's golf history. In an 11-year span from the 1984 Women's Kemper Open, through the 1995 ShopRite LPGA Classic, King won 30 times, including five major championships, to become the 14th member of the LPGA Hall of Fame and the first to cross the $5 million barrier in career earnings. She captured her sixth major in 1997, winning the Nabisco Dinah Shore.

King was born in Reading, Pa., and still maintains a home nearby in the town of Limekiln. She has served as host of the LPGA's CoreStates Betsy King Classic at Berkleigh C.C. in Kutztown, Pa., and has organized the Habitat for Humanity, which has built homes for underpriviliged families in Phoenix and Charlotte, N.C. In the off-season, she has traveled to Romania to work with an orphan relief organization, and she has been active in the Fellowship of Christian Athletes ministry since 1980.

Her favorite scripture is from 2 Corinthians: "Aim for perfection, listen to my appeal, be of one mind, live in peace. And the God of love and peace will be with you."

It was not easy for King to find peace when she first turned professional. Overshadowed by Nancy Lopez, and struggling with the pressure of great expectations — she finished eighth as an amateur in the 1976 U.S. Women's Open — King found salvation in the Bible and the golf instruction of Ed Oldfield. In 1984, she won three times, the LPGA money title and its Player of the Year Award. Her first major championship came in the 1987 Nabisco Dinah Shore, and two years later she had what was the most lucrative season in LPGA history. With six victories, including the U.S. Women's Open, King won $654,132. In those five years, her 20 victories were more than any professional golfer, man or woman, in the world.

Avoiding a letdown, King won her second Dinah and made it back-to-back Opens in 1990. Perhaps her most frustrating year came in 1993, when she won the Vare Trophy, the money title and Player of the Year honors, despite only winning one tournament, the season-ending Toray Japan Queens Cup. With the pressure of the Hall of Fame mounting (her 29 career victories left her one shy of induction), she was second five times that year, including the Dinah Shore and duMaurier, where she held third-round leads.

Shut out in 1994 for the first time in 10 seasons, King came back in 1995 with a final-round 67 at the Shoprite to qualify for the LPGA Hall. When she won the Dinah in 1997, it served as testimony of her perseverance. It was her third Dinah Shore, matching Amy Alcott's record, and her sixth major championship, tying her for sixth on the LPGA's all-time list with Kathy Whitworth and two of her more immediate contemporaries, Patty Sheehan and Pat Bradley.

"My faith gives me perspective," King says. "Scripture tells you to forget what is behind and press toward what is ahead, toward the goal to win the prize. The hardest thing is to forget what is behind. I use my faith as my sports psychologist. Why not get it from the guy who knows everything?"

THE KING RECORD

Major Championship Victories . . . 6
  U.S. Women's Open: 1989, 1990
  LPGA: 1992
  Nabisco Dinah Shore: 1987, 1990, 1997

LPGA Tour Victories 31

Vare Trophy: 1987, 1993

Leading Money Winner: 1984, 1989, 1993

Johnny Miller

In golf's modern era, it's commonly understood that no player has ever achieved the brief but memorable brilliance of Johnny Miller.

In 1974 and 1975, Miller won 12 tournaments. More important than the number of victories was the manner in which they were achieved, for during this streak Miller hit the ball consistently closer to the flag than any player in history. At his best, Miller's game was marked by incredibly aggressive and equally accurate iron play.

Miller won five of the first 11 events of 1974, and later three more. The next year, he won four. At Phoenix he shot 260 to win by 14. The next week at Tucson, he closed with a 61 to win by nine.

"It was sort of golfing nirvana," Miller said later. "I'd say my average iron shot for three months in 1975 was within five feet of my line, and I had the means for controlling distance. I could feel the shot so well."

This brilliant stretch was framed by Miller's most important victories. At the 1973 U.S. Open at Oakmont, he was six behind after a third-round 76 when he suddenly caught fire. He birdied the first four holes of the final round and continued to shoot at the flag. He made four more birdies against one bogey for a 63 to win by one. In the 1976 British Open at Royal Birkdale, Miller trailed 19-year-old Seve Ballesteros by two going into the final round, but put together a 66 to win by six.

That victory marked the end of Miller's reign at the top of the game, as he didn't win another tournament until 1980. Several factors contributed. Miller lacked the insatiable appetite for success that drives the very greatest. Bored with golf, Miller spent a summer working on his ranch and found that his stronger body could not repeat his old swing. Never a brilliant putter, Miller began to suffer from the yips. Finally, Miller's priorities changed the moment he had the first of his six children in 1977.

In all, Miller won 24 times on the PGA TOUR. His final and probably most remarkable victory occurred at Pebble Beach in 1994. Playing on one of his favorite courses, Miller somehow kept making putts—at times closing his eyes during the stroke—and won by a stroke.

Born in San Francisco April 29, 1947, Miller took up golf as boy under the watchful eye of his father, Larry. "I was very lucky because my father was always positive and never pushed," said Miller. "He always called me Champ." Later, Miller was guided by teacher John Geertson, who shaped Miller's distinctive early wrist cock takeaway. Miller received playing privileges at the Olympic Club, and in 1964 won the U.S. Junior Amateur. As a 19-year-old amateur, he qualified for the 1966 U.S. Open at Olympic and finished eighth.

He attended Brigham Young University and turned professional in 1969, nearly winning the 1971 Masters. After his victory at Oakmont, Miller got his biggest confidence boost by partnering Nicklaus in the World Cup. "I played every day with Jack for a week, and I started to believe that at that time, I was actually better than him." Nicklaus eventually answered Miller's challenge to his station as the game's best by outdueling Tom Weiskopf and him down the stretch at the 1975 Masters. "When I got to the mountaintop, I kind of looked at the scenery and and wondered, 'Now what?'" Miller once summarized. 'When Jack got there, he said, Where's the next mountain?'"

Since retiring from regular competition, Miller has become a popular television golf commentator.

THE MILLER RECORD

Major Championship Victories . . . 2
  U.S. Open: 1973
  British Open: 1976
Other Significant Victories
  U.S. Junior Amateur: 1964
PGA TOUR Victories 24
Ryder Cup Teams 2
  (2-2-2) 1975, 1981
Leading Money Winner: 1974

Nick Faldo

Like Ben Hogan before him, Nick Faldo seeks perfection with such singlemindedness that winning — much like the followthrough of his flawless swing — is only a byproduct of a larger goal.

More than any player of his era, the Englishman has relentlessly pursued golf's holy grail — total control of the golf ball. The swing he has built in that endless chase is one that has not only held up, but excelled, in the game's most important moments.

Between 1987 and 1995, Faldo won six major championships — three British Opens and three Masters. Although he has a total of 39 tournament victories around the world including six events on the PGA TOUR, Faldo's focus has always been on his performance in the Masters, U.S. Open, British Open and PGA Championship. In one stretch between 1988 and 1993, Faldo was never out of the top 20 in a Grand Slam event.

Faldo has relied on dedication, consistency, tempo and one of the strongest competitive minds the game has ever seen. Although he is tall at just over 6-3, and athletically built with wide shoulders, Faldo has never been a particularly powerful player. Consistency, distance control and course management are his strengths. His record makes him arguably the finest player of his height or taller in the history of the game.

Four of his majors were won narrowly in tense battles, either by a single stroke or in a playoff, and often after he had come from behind. At the 1987 British Open, Faldo made 18 pars in the final round and emerged victorious when Paul Azinger bogeyed the final two holes. At the 1989 Masters, he won in sudden death when Scott Hoch missed a 20-inch putt. The next year, Raymond Floyd mishit his approach on the second extra hole to give Faldo victory. In 1992 at Muirfield, Faldo lost a five stroke lead on Sunday, but rallied with late birdies to win his third British Open by one.

At the 1996 Masters, Faldo started the final day six strokes behind Greg Norman, but put together a flawless 67 to win going away. Faldo most impressive major victory was the 1990 British Open at St. Andrews. Mastering the Old Course with dazzling iron play, Faldo stood astride the field, shooting 18 under par 270 to win by five.

Born July 18, 1957, in Welwyn Garden City, England, Faldo was a gifted all-around athlete who had the makings of a first class cyclist. After his parents bought him a racing cycle when he was 12, the young Faldo horrified them by dismantling the whole machine because he wanted to know how it worked and insure that it was put together precisely. Years later, he would later do the same thing with his golf swing. At age 14, Faldo took up golf after watching the 1971 Masters on television. An early teacher, Ian Connelly, told him, "The easier you swing, the better you'll hit it," advice which helped shape Faldo's syrupy action through the ball.

Faldo won 10 titles in 1975 as an amateur and joined the European Tour the following season. Over the next eight years, he displayed a superb short game and putting stroke in winning several several tournaments establishing his career long brilliance in the Ryder Cup. But Faldo seemed to fail in the crucible of the major championships, and this did not sit well with his perfectionist nature. At the 1983 British Open at Birkdale, another final round collapse convinced Faldo that if he was ever going to win majors, he needed to overhaul his swing.

Enlisting swing coach David Leadbetter in 1984, Faldo implored the instructor to "Throw the book at me." For the next three years, he toiled through poor performance as he went through the rigors of a risky mid-career swing change. But the swing that emerged, which emphasized the large muscles of the body in comformance with Leadbetter's overriding tenet that "the dog wags the tail," was more solid, more repeatable and more reliable. Faldo's victory at Muirfield in 1987 was the validation, and the five majors that followed have been the proof.

THE FALDO RECORD

Major Championship Victories . . . 6
Masters: 1989, 1990, 1996
British Open: 1987, 1990, 1992
PGA TOUR Victories 6
European Tour Victories 26
Ryder Cup Teams 11
(23-19-4) 1977, 1979, 1981,
1983, 1985, 1987, 1989, 1991,
1993, 1995,1997